Natalie Baxter is a 32-year-old married woman, and a mother of three young children. She was born in Shrewsbury, but has lived most of her life in Colchester, Essex. She absolutely loves animals and has two dogs, two rabbits, one cat, and one hamster. Her dream is to open up a rescue home and help all animals in need. After working a few customer facing jobs, she eventually began to work for Royal Mail and loved the outdoors, independent, and active role she had. Unfortunately, due to her mother becoming unwell and needing more care, she had to give up her job and did what she does best and put her family first.

My mum Sue – Mum, you are an amazing woman, you have been given a cruel fate and deserve so much more. If I can help others that end up in my situation by writing our story, then at least something good has come out of this awful diagnosis. You are kind, loving and you're my best friend. You have been taken away from me far too soon. You inspire me to be a better person and to be the best version of myself. Thank you for being the best mum and for making me the person I am today.

Natalie Baxter

ONE TEAR AT A TIME

AUSTIN MACAULEY PUBLISHERS™

LONDON * CAMBRIDGE * NEW YORK * SHARJAH

A CIP catalogue record for this title is available from the British Library.

ISBN 9781398424487 (Paperback)
ISBN 9781398424494 (ePub e-book)

www.austinmacauley.com

First Published 2023
Austin Macauley Publishers Ltd®
1 Canada Square
Canary Wharf
London
E14 5AA

Dad – you have encouraged me to write my feelings down from day one and have been by my side fighting this battle every step of the way. You have read my book, given me courage to push forwards with it and helped me get my book out for the world to see. Thank you for your support, not just with my book, but with everything. I cannot put into words how proud I am to call you my dad. You have shown me the true meaning of love, family and respect. I Love you.

Table of Contents

Foreword   11

Introduction   13

Who am I?   15

The Lady She Was   19

Early Warning Signs   25

The Diagnosis   35

Our First Dementia Meeting   38

The Downhill Decline and Deterioration   41

Our Battle with The People We Couldn't See   46

The Accusations and Questions of Trust   55

A Break in The Chain of Routine   61

Mental Health Hospital 1 Added Accusations, Anxiety, Anger and
Absent Belongings   73

The Review   80

Medication Is Given to Help, Right?   86

Out of The Frying Pan And Into The Fire   94

Whilst The Cats Away The Mice Will Play   101

The Care Amended, the Disease Degraded   109

The Fine Line Between Love and Hate   115

Mental Health Hospital 2 History Repeated, Inadequately Treated,
Feeling Defeated   121

The Inevitable Final Breakdown   132

A Stepping Stone to Her New Found Home   141

She Deserved the Best, We Hoped For Good, She Got 'Outstanding'   156

The Obstacles of The Past, Present and Future   176

My World Comes Crashing Down   189

The Last Time We Say Goodbye   197

The Conclusion The Good, The Bad, and The Ugly   209

My Eternal Appreciation   222

Foreword

Natalie came to see me one morning in June 2019 at the care home. Alderwood is a care home in Colchester where we specialise in dementia, residential and nursing care, and I am also the manager.

I came out of my office to meet Natalie and I saw this young woman sitting with her head down on the sofa with such sadness in her eyes. She appeared to be the same age as one of my daughters and I immediately just wanted to give her a hug as I would my own daughter, but I thought that wouldn't have been appropriate at that time. The look on her face was of a mixture between lost, sad, anger and disbelief that she was having to do this, so I sat with her and asked as I do in my role as manager of the home, to tell me what had brought her to me that day and how I could help. She went on to say that her mum had dementia at only 55 years old! (younger than me I thought.) I found it hard to hold back the emotions I felt and that this young woman sat in front of me could have been one of my daughters having to deal with this. I could see that this nightmare situation was taking an immense toll on this family and that Natalie, who has three young children to care for just like my own daughter, was only just about coping. She was very fragile yet staying strong for her mum, now that's love for you, and at this point I thought Susan must have been the best mum. Natalie was doing her very best by fighting for the best care for her mum and I was in total admiration for her for doing that. I had an indescribable feeling of empathy for Natalie, her dad Tony (Susan's husband) and all the family.

Natalie told me from the beginning about the situation she was in now where her mum was in a care home and she just felt helpless, despite going in every day to check her mum was OK. I could see it was soul destroying to see her mum just walking around aimlessly with no emotions, just head down, talking to herself and thinking people were following her. Natalie explained how her mum appeared frightened, unhappy, alone and all the residents were so much older than Susan with also varying degrees of dementia.

Natalie just kept on saying, "I want the best for my mum, where she is safe, happy and well cared for." She wanted to see her smile again interacting with the family rather than being on edge all the time. I felt so sad for Natalie and immediately thought we have got to help Susan and this family. I knew a room had just become available but I had to follow the procedure to go and assess Susan, as my duty of care to make sure we could meet her needs and make a difference. I knew we could improve her quality of life. Natalie's face lit up when I revealed the news to her and I could see a weight had been lifted.

I went to see Susan in her care home and I felt so sad (hiding my emotions again), but I tried to keep it relaxed for Susan and the family. I knew immediately that this lovely lady needed more support, and not medication to make her sleepy. Yes, her dementia is tragic but we can make a difference and get to know the Susan, the daughter, the mother, the wife and the grandmother before her dementia. With time, love, kindness and a place where Susan feels safe in our care home, we could make a difference for her and the whole family.

Once Susan moved in, what touched my heart was the heart and soul put into making it a home for her by her family. Natalie and her husband came in every evening to paint and decorate her room, they got a nice comfy double bed and a big relaxing chair. From the smaller details like her special heart-shaped cushion, some sparkly accessories and the walls adorned with family photos.

Susan was very lost at first when she came in, she would not eat or drink sitting down because she was constantly moving. We would walk with her at mealtimes with food and drink in our hands hoping she would trust us, and she eventually did. It is now a joy to see her eating in the dining areas with the other residents. We now see Susan has the care and support she needs for a woman in her 50s, she gets her hair done, her nails painted and we can see her true personality. She smiles, sings, dances and chats to everyone. She teaches us new dance moves when the music that is playing in the home most days is on. Susan is always bopping along to the music with a smile, getting the staff to join, such a lovely sight to see. Some days she can be a little withdrawn but we just keep being there for her, never giving up.

No, we can't take the dementia away, we but we can make life better!

This book is a deep and sad insight into this awful disease and how it affects those around it. Well worth the read and I am sure it will answer many questions for people that read it.

Nikki

Introduction

I wrote this book as a way of coping but also as a way of possibly helping others that have to go through what I have, so that they know they are not alone. As some things have happened I have written them down but I have also found that just writing from the heart, as and when it feels right for me, helps to keep this book genuine and with all the emotion as I am going through it. In my busy and consumed life, it gives me time to sit back and reflect and also makes me remember what horrific disease my mum is facing and the reality of the situation. I'm currently writing this book whilst still facing the downhill battle that is Alzheimer's with my mum. If you would have told me that I would be going through all this in my life at 30, I would have struggled to believe you. She was diagnosed at only 55 and I would have thought she was far too pleasant, gentle and loved to go through one of the most hideous and distressing diseases there is, in my opinion. There have been days I have wished it could have been anything else. ANYTHING! Just not this, anything but this.

I had heard of Alzheimer's many times but just never thought it would strike my family, especially at such a young age with my mum. I thought Alzheimer's was something you got when you were old, and that is why I never really gave it much thought. Life drifts by with little knowledge about this awful disease that affects many people, then all of a sudden it curses your family member and you learn more and more as each day passes. It grips your entire life because it has taken hold of your loved one. It grips them harder and harder and with each grip it takes a layer of them away with it, until you're left with the shell of a person. I say 'a person' because they are not the person you knew, they change as a person, their habits, likes and dislikes, their personality, EVERYTHING. This disease not only takes away your loved one piece by piece but I feel like I am losing a part of myself along the way too. A huge part of my life is my mum, but not in the way it should be. It's now about caring for her and trying to keep things as 'normal' as they can be for as long as they can be. I don't get to enjoy her and her company the way I did before. It also takes over my personality sometimes. I can be very short tempered and snappy because she hasn't had a great day or my dad's struggling to cope and I'm trying to be a daughter, carer, mother, wife and have time for myself and it's all tainted by thoughts of how angry I am at my mum being handed a death sentence. A death sentence that is prolonged with agony and hurt. Alzheimer's takes your loved one away from you like a tsunami rips through a town, causing devastation along the way. You try to carry on and try to continue with your other roles in life but it's so hard. This book is my very real account of my life whilst caring for my mum with Alzheimer's. My emotions are real, the fall outs are real, and every single word I have written is from the heart.

My mum was diagnosed with early onset Alzheimer's in January 2018 and it has been the worst time of my life so far. Happy times tainted and my life consumed with caring, crying, planning and hoping. This is my honest and open interpretation of dealing with Alzheimer's first hand and the effects it has as it's happened.

Who am I?

My name is Natalie and when I began writing this book I was 32 years old, I have an older brother and a younger sister. I have always been the 'soft' one and the one that gets emotional a lot easier. Sometimes I have thought that I'm the weak one in the family who gets easily upset and hates confrontation, but after the last couple of years of my life I've realised I'm not weak. Being emotional and getting upset does not make me weak, and not wanting to argue or upset people doesn't make me the weak link. One thing I have proven to myself and probably my family is if anything I am strong, and coping with the amount of pressure and upset that I have faced has made me stronger. Dealing with my mum and caring for her daily has made me face challenges I never thought I would. I honestly feel like I've been so lucky with my parents. I look up to them both, my mum is the kindest most loving lady ever, and my dad has the biggest heart and he will do anything for anybody.

I am married and a mother to 3 children. My oldest Tommy is 6 and he is the gentlest, kindest most loving little boy. He's the apple of my dad's eye and they have such a close bond that I'm very proud of. He looks up to my dad and loves spending time with him. Millie is 5 years old. She is intelligent, inquisitive, loving and eager to learn new things. She is also 5 going on 15 and can be a stroppy little madam when she feels in the mood to push my buttons. Millie picks up on things going on around her and changes that are occurring. She was the first one to question Nanny's 'strange' behaviour and would ask me, 'why is nanny talking to herself?' or 'why does she keep repeating herself?' My youngest, Charlotte, is an absolute dream. She is now 2 years old and has been the easiest most laid-back baby. She's a bundle of happiness and I truly believe we had her at the right time. She's been my ray of sunshine on the darkest days, my reason to smile when all I have wanted to do is cry and the way my mum's eyes light up when she is around Charlotte is a memory I shall cherish forever. I was pregnant with Charlotte when my mum was diagnosed with Alzheimer's and she has been with me through most of the rocky journey.

My 3 children test me at times but I love them dearly and couldn't imagine life without them. My husband, Shaun, has been the rock that I have needed and he has never once complained. We work brilliantly as a team and he does everything he can to make my life easier, including helping with the children or helping with my family. He's left work early to help me with my mum, or to take over with the kids so I can concentrate on helping my mum. He helps with the cooking, cleaning and childcare and I really could not have coped with all this without him and he has enabled me to be there for my family as much as I have. He hasn't once made me feel like I have abandoned him even though my life has been consumed with my parents' health and wellbeing. I have said it before and I will say it over and over again, as far as I'm concerned my mum and dad need me right now, my life comes second. As long as my kids are loved and happy, then sharing my time is the best I can do right now. I have hopefully got years to make happy memories, my mum needs my efforts too. We also have a puppy, a dog, a cat, two rabbits and a hamster. So on top of caring for the children we have animals to love and care for, can't ever be said that we have an easy life.

I used to work at Royal Mail doing some computer work in the evenings. I was on maternity leave for the most part of my mum's illness but eventually I had to go back. I was only back to work for about a month when I decided I needed to quit work to concentrate on her care. This wasn't a decision I made lightly but a decision that was right for me at the time. Alzheimer's has changed my life forever and it isn't just my job I have lost.

The Lady She Was

My mum was born in 1963 in Manchester. She grew up with her mum, dad, and two sisters and lived a relatively normal childhood I believe. Her dad raised her from a very young age but she never knew her biological father as he left when she was just a baby. My mum never speaks much of her childhood but I do know that she has always seen the man that brought her up, my grandad, as her dad. She told me a few stories of her life before I was born but she never really spoke about the period of time before she met my dad. I always found it a bit strange, but it felt like maybe there was something she didn't want to talk about?

She met my dad when she was in school, about aged 14. Since getting together they have always been inseparable. They got married in 1984 before having their first baby together. Three children later, their family was complete. My dad was in the army so we moved around a lot, and my mum did a fantastic job of raising us whilst he was away. They eventually settled in Colchester, many miles away from family. My mum was used to being away from her family because of all the moving around and it didn't seem to bother her, as long as she had my dad she had everything she needed. She spoke to her mum once a week on the phone and would go to Manchester to visit maybe once a year.

My mum and dad have such a special relationship. For as long as I can remember they have always done everything together. They socialised together, were very affectionate, never really argued, and showed nothing but love for each other. A love to be admired. Seeing the way my parents were as a couple made me who I am today. It would take a special man to win my heart because I wanted a man that treated me the way my dad treated my mum, he was always a gentleman and always put her first. He would go without if it meant his family were happy. He really is my hero and all men should treat woman the way my dad does. He's an old-fashioned gentleman but also a modern-day man that did all the housework, meals, and would look after my mum the way she deserved when he was home. I am not saying he is Mr Perfect, but he was my mum's Mr Perfect, and who is perfect anyway?

After having their three children and once we were in school my mum started childminding. She was so good at her job, she was kind, caring and the children loved her. She dealt with the stress of children well and kept us occupied whilst also maintaining a house. After finally giving up the childminding she became a cleaner, riding a bike in the mornings to the house that she cleaned and then coming home at lunch time. She has always worked hard and been a role model for me. She really is kind, thoughtful and the most conscientious person I know.

One of my mum and dad's favourite things to do was cruise. My mum has always been claustrophobic so she would never get on a plane, therefore she turned to cruising. I remember when she went on her first cruise with my dad, and although she got severe sickness, she loved it. She would be out on the deck catching the sun rays every day and then enjoying the exquisite food and luxury spa. My dad would go to the gym whilst she was sunbathing or getting her nails painted. Then they would go to a coffee shop and get a coffee and hot chocolate, get lunch, enjoy evening dinner and go to the evening theatre shows together. My dad likes to venture off when the cruise docks and explore the countries they were lucky enough to visit, but my mum would be happy to stay on the ship or get off but not go too far. She is a very homely lady and likes her home comforts. Every time my dad got a taste for foreign countries he would suggest moving abroad one day but she just let it go over her head, as there was no way she was going to ever leave her home and her family.

I was lucky enough to go on several cruises with my mum and it always reminded me of how alike we were. We spent hours and hours laying on sun loungers soaking up the sun and we were both in our element. Our ideas of the perfect holiday are identical, lots of sunbathing and relaxing, lots of lovely food and then watching a fantastic show. We would then go to bed at about 9.30pm. We are both woman of routine, we are both early birds and we both love getting a tan. If it rained we would feel lost, not knowing what to do with ourselves, then realising the downside to being in the middle of a large ocean on a boat. Myself and my mum would get on like a house on fire, it was like being away with my best friend. Any countries that we had already visited we would decide to stay on the boat rather than getting off and walking around the unknown. We are both not the most adventurous and also both get anxious in situations that are not part of our everyday lives. So we would stick with what we knew best and sunbathe on deck whilst the ship was docked.

When my brother was hit with a mental health issue around 2005 it really hit us hard as a family. My mum didn't cope very well. She got put on anti-depressants and hit a very low point in her life. My dad also struggled but as a team they were as strong as ever. It really was like nothing could come between them and they could get through anything as long as they had each other. After a few years battling with my brother's mental health until he eventually got his own place, my mum's mental health plateaued. She took her medication daily and it kept her balanced.

Then a few years after that my mum and dad were involved in a fatal road traffic accident. They were on their way back from Manchester, when a car driver lost control and then got hit by a speeding van driver. If my dad wasn't doing a very sensible speed that day, he would have been involved in the pile up. He parked his car to the side and got out to help the young driver that had been hit. Unfortunately, although he gave it his best efforts, the trauma was too much and the young man died in my dad's arms. My mum stayed in the car and just panicked but it still affected her massively. She wouldn't like to travel if snow was predicted and she was much more aware of the dangers on the road. My dad's army related PTSD was triggered by this incident and he had to get help to cope with this. He could be OK one minute and then angry and snappy the next. My mum was very good at dealing with my dad and his moods, just as my dad was great at dealing with her nervous deposition and anxiety. Another show of what a great team they were and the reason they have been such a strong couple for so many years.

When the first grandchild came along my mum was so pleased and had such a special bond with her. My sister's daughter was born in February 2012. She loved spending time with her and even helped look after her from time to time, she was so happy to have a granddaughter. She would take her on a bus ride into town, play with her and even just chat about absolutely anything with her. Things that I now look back on and think if only that could happen now, the simple things that we take for granted. My mum really doted on her granddaughter and was delighted to see her and care for her anytime. This delight wasn't going to continue for too long and their connection was going to dissolve before our very eyes.

My mum started showing definite signs that something wasn't quite right in 2016. However, after the diagnosis in January 2018, I believe the signs were there a few years before. That was the start of the disease but at the time it wasn't obvious enough to think something was wrong.

Early Warning Signs

One of the biggest lessons that I have learned and that I would tell others is to follow your gut feeling. Don't be pushed to the side or fobbed off, if you feel something isn't right then pursue it until you are satisfied with the explanation you are given. It's your family member or friend and you know them better than any professional, so take the advice but follow your heart.

My mum was showing many signs of memory loss a few years before diagnosis but some of it started off so small that it was brushed aside. I mean even I worry about my memory sometimes, forgetting what I'm doing next or misplacing keys, etc. We all have memory lapses and forget things from time to time. However, I started noticing something wasn't right when it was becoming too frequent and other things started happening too.

She started repeating herself several times. She could tell me that she had been to Costa that morning, and then she would tell me again, and again and again. This could have been in the space of 5 minutes. She started to have to write everything on the calendar otherwise she wouldn't remember. We used to meet every day to walk the dogs in a lane about 5 minutes from her house. It would take her about 10 minutes at a slow pace, but she remembered her way there to begin with. However, whilst walking around the woods she would say to me, 'we haven't been this way before,' and yet we had walked this route in the woods hundreds of times. She was so disorientated she didn't really know where she was. My mum had always used her emails and loved internet shopping, however it got to the point where she couldn't remember passwords or how to do the internet shopping. One day I got a call off her and she was crying down the phone very distressed. She explained to me that she was on her internet banking and she was overdrawn. She was so upset because she always managed the money so well. My dad never had any input, she was always in control of the money going in and coming out. I asked her if she would like me to go round to help her and she said yes. So I jumped in the car with Charlotte who was only a few months old and went round to help. When I got there my mum was really distraught, so I had a look at her banking and saw her balance. She wasn't overdrawn and she had enough money in the account. I tried to explain what the figures meant and how to understand her balance but all I did was confuse her even more. From that moment on, I got several calls over the next few days asking for help with her banking and forgotten passwords. She would get so upset and I could see she was getting distressed because she had used the internet banking for years and never had any problems. It was confusing her and making her anxiety go through the roof. I told my dad something wasn't quite right and he told me to take charge of the internet banking and I also gave him a quick lesson on how to use it, as I felt he should know and have some input as it was his money.

My mum's anxiety starting getting quite bad. She would get stressed going to the supermarket, and would feel like she was lost if she wasn't right next to someone. Then another moment, that again rang alarm bells. She went to use her bank card to pay for her shopping and couldn't remember what to do. She stared blankly at her bank card and I told her to just tap her card on the pin machine and she got all flustered and said, 'I don't know what to do.' So I tapped the card for her. One of the most frustrating things when I went out with my mum was that people would stare at her when she would get in the way, or when she stood right in the middle of an aisle, or when she stood there not helping me pack her shopping. She would try to order the right drink for herself and my dad in Costa and she would stutter and get confused and then say I can't remember, before then paying and just walking off without saying thank you. She would come across rude but little did anybody know that she wasn't being rude but she was just so overwhelmed that everything that comes natural to us took a back seat, and that included manners.

My mum always had an issue with my sister being spoilt, she believed my dad let her get away with things she shouldn't be. She was always the one to say no when my sister wanted anything but my dad would say yes. She would moan to me about this and tell me that my sister always got her own way and needed to grow up. However, once the Alzheimer's symptoms started showing she was being much more harsh with the words she used about my sister. She would tell me she hated her, which was not like my mum to say, and ring me crying because my dad had lent her money. She would cry getting all confused about the amount borrowed and when it would get paid, and I would try to explain that it was fine and not to worry. She always had a good head on her shoulders in regards to money and decency, knowing when we needed to work for money or if we deserved it or not. With the disease she became a little bit more selfish, not wanting to treat anybody to anything. Even buying a hot drink for myself or my sister would annoy her, and this was totally out of character because she is the kindest most generous person I know.

Once we had the diagnosis there were a few more signs years before, that were ignored at the time but looking back they were definitely early signs of the Alzheimer's. So even before the memory loss and confusion, we noticed a few changes in my mum's behaviour. At the time we put it down to the menopause, but we now believe they were very early signs of Alzheimer's. When my sister's daughter was about 2 she began to lose interest. She didn't appear to be bothered if she saw her or not, she didn't pay her much attention and she didn't ever ask to see her. She was so in love with her granddaughter for the first two years of her life but the connection just seemed to slowly fade.

There's another event that really sticks in my head and looking back, I feel guilty about how I reacted. My mum and dad had been on a 17-night cruise, so we hadn't seen them for a very long time. At this moment in time I had my eldest Tommy and my oldest daughter Millie, she was only a baby. My dad rang me and asked if I had any potatoes in so they could have a jacket potato for dinner. On his way home he came by my house and dropped my mum off to come and collect them. Unfortunately, it didn't surprise me that my dad didn't come in or say hello because he could be a bit anti-social sometimes depending on his mood, so that was pretty normal. However, my mum walked through the front door, stood at the stairgate right in front of the kids, and waited for me to get the potatoes for her. She didn't once acknowledge the children, or even say hello. I gave her what she came for and then as she turned to head out I said, 'Are you not even going to say hello to your grandchildren?'

She looked all flustered and then said, 'Oh OK,' and went to turn to come back in, but I showed her the front door and told her not to bother. It really upset me that I had to prompt her to acknowledge my children after not seeing them for so long. I just thought she didn't care if she saw them or not and I have always hated having to tell people how to behave when it comes to general care and decency. When she got to the car with my dad she was apparently in tears and very upset. I got an email from my dad that night telling me I had upset my mum and that I should not have pushed her out the house. I argued that I didn't push her and she had exaggerated my hand guiding her out of my house, but he said for me to stay away from their house. Obviously this was resolved quickly because as a family it's rare that we fall out with each other for long, but I was still really upset by the whole thing. My mum was behaving like she didn't really care much about the children and I was thinking any "normal" nana would have missed their grandkids after more than a few weeks away. Ignoring anybody is rude and this rudeness upset me greatly. I was so hurt that my children must have meant so little to her and it felt like their existence didn't really matter. Little did I know back then that this was an early sign of the Alzheimer's, not my mum not caring. She was the most gentle caring lady and it was just so out of character, so we were putting these changes in personality down to the menopause initially.

I also took my mum along to an aerobics class one time. I asked her if she would like to go and she was very keen, saying that she did aerobics when she was younger and knew how to do it. When we got there and it started, I wanted the ground to swallow me up. She was in her own world and couldn't follow the simplest of steps. She was dancing around the floor and making moves up as she went along. People were laughing because they thought my mum was being comical and just enjoying herself, it was like she was purposely making up her own routine, but she wasn't. Her brain really could not cope with the simplest of instructions. They even joked at the end about my mum enjoying herself and having a great time, whilst joking and laughing. It was another of those situations where when I look back I think if only I knew I would have been a lot more helpful and not so embarrassed. Before the diagnosis, I use to get so frustrated with her. I spent so much time with her, that even half an hour with her repeating herself all the time, I would allow it a few times and then I would snap, 'You have told me that already, Mum.' I'm not the most patient of people and one thing you need when dealing with a disease like Alzheimer's is patience. My dad would do it too. He would try to be as patient as possible and then he would get annoyed at her, something we look back on and think if only we knew what was happening at that time.

One weekend a few years before the diagnosis, myself, my dad and my sister went to Wales to climb Snowdon. We had spoken about doing it for quite a while so one weekend we planned to travel on the Saturday morning, climb the mountain and then go home the next day. My mum said she didn't want to go as exercise had never been her favourite thing to do, so she stayed at home with the dog. I told her that Shaun, my husband, would take her to Costa with the kids and would take her out to the shops, etc. She was happy with staying and I knew Shaun would look after her and make sure she got out of the house as she couldn't drive. However, on the Saturday afternoon, when we were climbing Snowdon, we got several calls from family in Manchester. When we answered, they asked us why we had left our mum at home and that she was really upset. We were all so shocked because she had always stayed at home when we went to do any sort of physical activity because she didn't enjoy it. So for her to get upset and be really distressed being on her own wasn't normal. This was another early warning sign that we didn't realise was anything serious. I don't know if she forgot that we had told her where we were going but she really was troubled about being left. We thought it was strange but we just rang our mum and told her we would be home soon and she was OK with that. So we just brushed the whole incident aside thinking nothing more of it and put it down to her being a bit of a drama queen and emotional sometimes.

My mum for quite a few years had always bulk bought items in the house. She would buy three toothpastes because they were on offer and five shower gels. I also did this sometimes but just not to the extent that she did, however, it didn't stop there. She loved internet shopping for years and years and it got to the point where I found it funny because she would buy new bikinis every time she went on holiday. Not just one bikini but about six. Then she would buy new dresses and tops, and most of them wouldn't even get worn. I just thought my mum loved shopping and she had the money to do it so why not, but looking back there was definitely more to it than that. I believe she was buying stuff and not realising and maybe forgetting how much she had already bought. My dad was oblivious because he never involved himself with the money or what my mum was spending it on. I don't think even I knew how bad it was until after diagnosis, I just thought she spent too much money on clothes because she loved shopping.

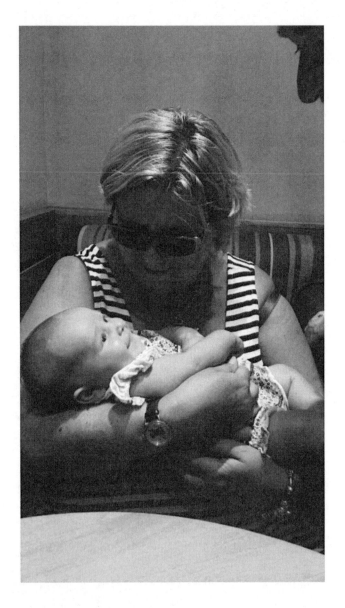

After diagnosis I cleared her spare room out, including all the wardrobes. I was astounded by the sheer volume of unnecessary items piled high in every little bit of available space. This included about ten shower curtains, ten packs of duvet sets, ten fitted sheets, twenty bikini sets with the tags in, about ten dresses with the tags in and so much more. There were a few brand-new coats and jackets and also some kids clothes that would no longer fit any of the children. My mum had obviously purchased items she saw and thought they would like and forgot about it. She also loved a fit flop style of shoe and had about six boxes of brand-new fit flops that do not come cheap. I think even if I had known the extent of what she was buying I still wouldn't have put that down to Alzheimer's without any other obvious clues. I would have just thought that she had money and she liked to spend it, she doesn't work and doesn't drive so it's her guilty pleasure and it passes the day.

Before the diagnosis of Alzheimer's, we went on an emotional rollercoaster. My mum had a sleep study done because we knew she was holding her breath when asleep. Initially we got told she didn't have sleep apnoea but then eventually we got the results back from the sleep study and we were told that she had severe sleep apnoea. She was given a mask to wear at night time to help her breathe, something my mum wasn't too keen on due to her claustrophobia and hating things over her face. When we first went to the doctors about her memory, it was all focused on her sleep apnoea as she was 'too young to get dementia.' She was referred to a specialist and again we were told she was too young for dementia and that sleep apnoea also causes memory loss. Initially we accepted that, but it didn't take long for me to think it was more than sleep apnoea. My mum had a brain scan in December 2016 and did a memory test, however, the focus was still on the sleep apnoea rather than anything else. My dad went to one meeting with a consultant and to his absolute disbelief he was wrongly informed that my mum had dementia because her family history showed that it ran in the family. My dad angrily stopped the consultant in his tracks and said, 'Can you make sure you know what you're talking about before you mention the word dementia, as dementia does not run in the family!' It turned out that alarmingly the consultant was looking at the wrong records. My dad was furious, had a few choice words and ended up getting told to leave the hospital. That was the last time my dad attended an appointment that wasn't at home because he just could not cope emotionally and knew his PTSD would surface.

Months went by and my mum was getting worse and worse. As explained it went from simple memory loss and repetitiveness to forgetting daily activities that she usually did with ease like banking, shopping and dog walking routes. I knew by this point that there was more to this than just sleep apnoea so I continued to question her symptoms and wasn't going to accept any answers that were not definitive. A whole year on a slow decline the professionals finally agreed to look into it further, they did another brain scan and another memory test. They said they could compare the tests with the ones completed the year before. After a few weeks, we were waiting for the results and nothing. I kept phoning and was told I would get a call back, but never did. My sister was chasing for the results too, we were both ringing and getting no joy. Eventually I managed to get through to the right person and was finally given a time and date to go and see the consultant with the results. It was a relief but also filled me with fear and anxiety because I knew that day could change our lives forever.

The Diagnosis

The day my mum was given a diagnosis of Alzheimer's is a day I will never ever forget. It is still so clear in my mind and the emotions I felt are still so memorable. I still have days now two years later where I think about it and it upsets me because that was the day that tipped our lives upside down. It was decided that I would take her to the meeting with the consultant and I was feeling very apprehensive and worried about what the outcome would be. I was also over halfway through my pregnancy with Charlotte and feeling extra emotional with my hormones all over the place. My mum didn't seem to be too stressed about the meeting, in fact she seemed relatively calm. We sat in the waiting room waiting to be called in and I felt sick to my stomach, I was sat twiddling my fingers and trying to convince myself that she was far too young for dementia and it had to be something else. I think deep down I knew that I was going to hear something I didn't want to because I knew there had to be more to my mum's behaviour. When we got called in, we sat down and were introduced to the consultant. He explained that my mum had undertaken two brain scans and two memory tests a year apart and this was a good indication of what was going on. I could sense from his apprehension and emotive look on his face that he had bad news to give. He took a long slow pause and then expressed that he was really sorry but it did look like some form of dementia. At that moment in time I felt like someone had ripped my heart out, stood on it, and then placed the crumpled mess back in my chest. My world had just been tipped upside down and I had to try to understand how to place it back into some form of normality. My mum cried and seemed quite upset but still to this day I don't think she realised what this diagnosis meant for her. To be totally honest I didn't realise the extent of the journey that we would all have to face as a family, and how tough it was going to be.

If I'd have known that day what the next year was going to hold I would have probably sunk into a dark place because the distress and destruction the disease creates is far more than I could have ever imagined. When asked what dementia meant for her, my mum said it meant she had a bad memory and forgot things. The consultant went on to explain that he believed the type of dementia she had was Alzheimer's. He did try and explain why he had come to this decision but I was so taken aback by what I had just been told I wasn't really listening. It was all a blur because the word dementia just kept going round and round my head, I couldn't concentrate fully on anything else. I'm not somebody that shows my emotions in front of people unless I really can't help it, I like to hide how I feel so that I don't appear weak. I just remember turning my head down to the side and my eyes filling up, and the tears streaming down my face. I couldn't hold them back, no matter how much I tried. I just kept thinking what my dad was going to think about the diagnosis. How would I tell him? How was he going to cope?

The consultant went on to explain that the memory section of the brain had shrunk on the second scan, and that there was a decrease on the second memory test. He said that he thought medication should be started to try to slow down the dementia even though he could not say with 100% certainty that it was dementia. I asked him to clarify because we didn't want to have any glimmer of hope that shouldn't have been there, and he said it looks to be dementia with all the evidence present. He sounded pretty certain but clarified that he could never be one hundred percent certain at this stage. He said it would have no harmful effects to start the medication and see what happened from there. He believed the sleep apnoea was preventing my mum from getting the right diagnosis as it does cause memory loss but he said he doesn't believe it would be causing everything she was experiencing. He gave us some leaflets and asked if we had any questions, but I think we were so numb from what we had heard I couldn't really think of any. Being about 20 weeks pregnant makes you emotional anyway but sitting and trying to process a diagnosis of a disease that we all know has no cure with the extra hormones, was beyond devastating.

Once we had left the memory centre I got my mum into the car, whilst I stood outside for a few minutes contemplating what to do next. My dad was waiting for us in the Costa five minutes up the road so I decided to ring my sister and told her what had happened. We both had a cry and then I said I needed to go because I needed to break the news to our dad and tell him what had happened. I was devastated by this earth-shattering news we just received and I was nervous about telling my dad. I knew he would be upset which would make me even more upset than I already was. I wanted to be strong but knew on this occasion there was just no chance, I didn't want to cry with anybody watching me and would have much preferred to ping my dad an email with the crushing news. I don't do face to face emotion, I like to be hard faced and cry behind closed doors. However, I am such an emotional person that I get upset very easily, especially when it comes to my family. So the whole way to Costa in the car I was trying to hold it together, but my plan went to pieces before I even got there. We pulled up in the car and my dad was in Costa so I rang him and told him to come outside. There was no way I was crying in a public place with an audience. As soon as he came near the car I turned into a crumpled mess and told him it wasn't good news. I told him the words he was hoping and praying he would not have to hear, Mum had dementia. My dad looked like he had been punched sideways in the stomach, he looked in pain. He went over to my mum who again had started crying and he gave her a hug. He said not to worry and that we could get through it. He dealt with it surprisingly well but I don't think he realised the extent of the diagnosis at that moment. He knew it was bad, but not as bad as the next year was going to prove to be. We stopped crying, went for an eerily quiet drink in Costa and then across to the pharmacy to pick up the new medication she was prescribed to slow down the dementia. We dealt with the diagnosis as well as we could but from that moment things went from bad to worse very quickly.

Our First Dementia Meeting

A few weeks later we had our first dementia meeting with somebody that could answer any of our questions and do some basic evaluation of my mum's current condition. A lady that was part of the dementia team performed numerous tests on my mum asking questions and getting her to perform some simple tasks. She was also there to give us any information we needed and make sure I understood what a dementia diagnosis meant. She asked my mum some basic details including her name and date of birth, both of which she was able to answer without any help. However, when the lady asked what year it was, she couldn't answer because she didn't know. She asked my mum to copy simple sentences and again she struggled. You could see her brain just couldn't process what she had to do, something so simple was so difficult and stressful. For example repeating the straightforward sentence, 'and, if, but.' She would forget the last word or the order they were said in. The lady asked her to draw a simple object and she couldn't. Putting pen to paper proved difficult and processing the image she was asked to draw from brain to hand was almost impossible. She was then instructed to copy a few simple hand actions. So for example, she was shown a hand cutting the other, a hand slapping the other and a hand thumping the other in a sequence. She couldn't work out which hand to make into which shape and what was supposed to be straightforward was actually really difficult. She just kept staring at her hands and trying to move them in the correct way but would do something completely different. My mum was looking defeated and agitated at herself for being unable to do what was asked of her, but the lady was very good with her. She didn't put pressure on her or make her feel like she was doing anything wrong. She made us both laugh and made my mum feel like she was doing as well as anybody else in her situation would do. She explained to us that they had groups on every week for cognitive brain therapy so that my mum could try and stimulate her brain a bit more. She explained that each week they did activities at the centre and numerous people attended. She told us that we could chat to other people going through the same thing which might help us get an idea of what was to come. She also informed us of some other groups that family could go to if they wanted to talk to others or get help and advice. I felt like it was a nice idea but I knew that talking to a group of strangers wasn't going to be something my dad and I were going to take onboard just yet. We were only just trying to get our own heads around my mum's diagnosis and I knew I didn't have the emotional capability to talk to others when I didn't really want to accept it was happening.

After a few minutes and as the meeting was drawing to a close my mum needed to go to the toilet. Whilst one lady took her to the toilet, I used the opportunity to ask some questions I didn't want to ask in front of her. My dad had told me to ask a specific question that he felt he needed to know the answer to but one that felt a bit dark for the stage we were at. I felt so wrong for asking the question but when you are not aware what the future holds you need answers to help you deal with what's to come. So I asked, 'What is the life expectancy of somebody of my mum's age with Alzheimer's.' The lady looked at me and told me that every case was different. She explained that some people have 3 years from diagnosis and some people have 23 years. There's no telling what will happen as not one person is the same. I started to feel slightly positive hoping that my mum could fight this for many years yet but then she crashed all my hopes in one sentence. She stated that generally people that get diagnosed earlier in life tend to deteriorate quicker. When she said that to me, it rang alarm bells in my heart because I knew my mum was very young at 54 to be diagnosed but at the same time I felt like she couldn't be that unlucky. I just kept thinking she was too young, happy and loved to get such a cruel disease and then for it to rapidly take hold. I held onto the hope that some people have a lot longer than others and my mum would be one of the luckier ones. Little did I know that what I was told that day about rapid deterioration in younger people, could not have been more true. She wasn't one of the luckier ones and in fact it seemed everything that could go wrong, did!

The Downhill Decline and Deterioration

A short while after diagnosis my mum was appointed a social worker. We had our first meeting with her and she ran over some details and answered any questions we had. Little did I know at that moment that we were blessed with an amazing social worker that was going to come to our rescue time and time again making our lives a little bit more bearable. If only she could see and understand the difference she made to our lives when we needed help, it's something my dad and I will always remember and appreciate. She also checked to see how my mum was getting on with the new medication and we explained that we had not seen any changes at that present time. Whilst she was visiting she also put into place for my mum to start the cognitive therapy sessions she was told about. She felt it would help with her memory and keep her mind active.

When my mum started going to the therapy sessions she wasn't over the moon about it as she was surrounded by a lot of old people and I think she found it quite boring. A few weeks after going to the therapy she started saying that people were being horrible and ignoring her and she had to sit in the corner on her own. We knew that she wasn't overjoyed about going to therapy and we thought maybe she was just being a bit sensitive or wanted to get out of going to any further sessions. That was just the start of her downward spiral and she started showing more signs of deterioration. Still to this day we don't know if it was how it was planned for my mum and nothing could change that or whether it was the new medication having an adverse effect on her and starting her downward spiral.

On the odd occasion my mum started wetting herself, it was rare but it was happening. Initially it seemed like she was not making it to the toilet on time and it was happening so rarely that it wasn't a massive issue. I knew that I had tried to hold a wee on several occasions and not quite made it in time, wetting myself a little. I'm sure we have all done this at some time or another, especially after giving birth, so it didn't feel like a big deal. However, it was only the beginning for my mum and this was going to become a very uphill battle for myself and my dad as things went from bad to worse.

About four months after diagnosis my parents went on a two-week cruise together. After about a week away, I got a call off my dad saying that my mum was getting really upset. He explained that she had gone to the toilet on the cruise and when she came out she was crying and said that somebody was being horrible to her. She was quite distressed and my dad was obviously concerned but he was quite sure that there was nobody else in the toilet as it was a one-person cubicle. My mum eventually calmed down but whatever had happened had caused her a substantial amount of concern and upset. When my dad explained all this to me, I couldn't really process what he was saying and my suggestion was that maybe something had happened and he was getting the wrong end of the stick. I said it didn't sound right and mum wouldn't be making it up. She must have believed what she was saying otherwise she wouldn't have got so upset. We sort of just moved on from what had happened because there was no explanation and it hadn't changed anything. My dad also explained on another phone call that she was getting lost on the ship quite a lot. My mum has never been very good with directions or knowing her way round places so again this didn't surprise me. However my dad was adamant it was different this time, he said she didn't even know how to get to the toilet on her own. Without my dad she wouldn't have had a clue where to go and would have been more confused and agitated. All in all they had a great holiday but once they were back home she went from bad to worse and the incident in the toilet on holiday all made sense.

I was sat at home one afternoon when I got a phone call off my dad who was very distressed. He didn't say much but just said that he thought my mum needed help and he got tearful and hung up. So I jumped into my car with Charlotte and drove straight round the corner to my dad's. When I got to their house he was stood outside with his dark shades and frown lines above them. He told me to go inside and see what was happening. This was said through tears because although he had dark shades I could hear this from his shaking voice. Them frown lines were to be something I would start seeing quite a bit of and they still to this day kill me inside because my dad doesn't get upset easily and he certainly doesn't let it show. If my dad's crying then I need to be seriously concerned. When I got inside the house, my mum was crying her eyes out, she was so upset and stressed she looked lost. I asked why she was crying and tried to reassure her that it was

OK because I was there now. She gave me a hug and said that they were being horrible. When I asked who they were she said 'them.' The people that lived in the house with her were being horrible and not letting her go to the toilet. She said they were being really nasty and that they were telling lies about her. I asked where they lived and she said they lived with her and my dad and that they were probably upstairs whilst we were talking. I was in complete shock. From seeing my mum being quite forgetful and repeating her words to now having lost all concept of reality was a very real worry for me. It broke my heart because it didn't matter what I said to her she really and truly believed that somebody else was living in her house and they were trying to control her and upset her. Now I've read numerous times that you're not supposed to disagree with anything said by somebody with dementia because they believe what they are saying, but even now I struggle with that. How do I agree with something that isn't true? It goes against everything I have ever been taught from a child. One thing I can always say and one thing I am proud of is my honesty. Now I understand that sometimes we have different situations that require us to adapt, but it's so hard when it goes against your natural instincts. My mum was shaking from her upset and was genuinely really put out by these "people". I told her it would be OK and that there was nobody else in the house apart from her and my dad. I was unaware that I was supposed to agree with what was being said at that point, so I did what came naturally and tried to reassure her. She just kept repeating what I was telling her, that there was nobody else there just her and dad over and over. It was like she was even trying to convince herself that this was the case even though she was very sure other people were living in the house.

Eventually she calmed down and seemed to become more settled, so I took her out for a walk just to take her mind off whatever had just happened. After that incident, I got onto the phone to the social worker to inform her of this sudden change in behaviour. There was no answer so I phoned the crisis number I was given for help and advice. I got through to a lady and I explained all the changes and what was happening. It was one of the hardest phone calls I had ever made because I didn't have a clue what was happening and I was scared. She was very reassuring and told me that it was possible that my mum may have had an infection. She told me that if I could I should try and get a urine sample and take it to the doctors to be checked. She explained that when people with dementia have an infection it can affect them quite badly in so many ways and will really impact their behaviour. I remember this day so clearly because when

I got on the phone to them I just burst into tears and struggled to get my words out because I was so shocked and upset by what was happening. It didn't feel like reality and it wasn't what I was expecting as part of the Alzheimer's. They calmed me down and made me feel like they could help, telling me to ring back if I couldn't get any help with the doctors. I rang the doctors and they got us in for an emergency appointment after some persuasion by myself. It's never easy to get an appointment at the doctors at the best of times but normally when you ring half way through the day you have to be very lucky to get an appointment. Normally I'm not very forceful with my words but this day was very different, when I'm concerned as much as I was I wasn't going to put that phone down until somebody could help us. The first thing they told me was that they wanted a urine sample to check for infection. They advised I used a sterile pot and got a sample to take with us to the appointment. I got a urine sample from my mum and off we went to the doctors to hopefully find out what the hell was going on. Myself and my dad were thinking this can't be how bad things have got already. We have years before things get this bad, there must be an explanation.

When we got to the doctors my mum was given a little health check. They checked her heart rate and blood pressure and also her temperature. Everything was coming back as normal, including the urine that was dipped. I was so disappointed and very confused because I knew if it was an infection, then some antibiotics would have made everything normal again and it would have explained this behaviour my mum was displaying. I asked the doctor what that meant and she began to ask my mum some questions, including why she was getting upset at home. My mum looked muddled and said, 'no I'm not I'm fine.'

So I then said, 'mum you're not fine, you were getting upset saying people in your house were being horrible and telling you that you couldn't go to the toilet.' She then unravelled in front of the doctor and couldn't hide her emotion any further. She was so upset and actually quite scared. She spoke through tears and explained that there were people in her house that lived with her and they were being nasty. They wouldn't let her go to the toilet and they were telling lies about her. When asked who these people were she got even more upset and said that they were called Sue and that they were wearing this (she pinched at the dress she was wearing and held it up).

Then she shouted out in quite an abrupt voice for somebody as calm and placid as my mum, 'it was her, she was horrible.' She exclaimed, 'I am horrible and I'm the nasty one!' It was quite obvious to myself and the doctor that my mum was very confused and not making much sense, but what was more obvious and clearer than anything else was that it was all very true and disturbing for her.

The doctor explained to me that the urine was fine and so were all her other observations. She told me that sometimes people with Alzheimer's have good days and bad days and they can also deteriorate very quickly. She went on to explain that it wasn't unknown of for somebody with Alzheimer's to be confused about their own identity or to be seeing or hearing somebody else that isn't actually there. So after a shocking day we didn't have any explanation and just felt like we had been pushed back several steps since the diagnosis. We just had to accept what had happened and cope with it. The social worker eventually rang me back and I explained what had happened, and she arranged to come and see my mum the next morning.

When the social worker came round, my mum behaved very sheepishly. She didn't want to reveal any of her thoughts and pretended like nothing had happened. When asked if she was OK she said, 'yes I'm fine' like the day before didn't exist. The social worker asked me what had happened and I explained everything from the day before. I still remember the look on my mum's face when I described the episode, she was looking at me with disappointment and betrayal. She wasn't happy that I was telling the social worker everything. When the social worker pressed her more about what happened, she still continued to deny everything until eventually she cracked. She explained that there were others in the house and they were not letting her go to the toilet. She got so upset and distressed that it was hard for me and my dad to see. However it also made us realise why she was wetting herself, because she wasn't allowed to go to the toilet. She said they were horrible, nasty and telling lies. When asked about who "they" were my mum got even more confused. She couldn't explain who they were, they were just the horrible people that lived in the house. My dad and I decided that the medication wasn't helping. She was deteriorating pretty rapidly and since starting the medication she was hallucinating. So between ourselves and the social worker we decided that we would look into stopping the medication that should be slowing the Alzheimer's and see how we go from there.

Our Battle with The People
We Couldn't See

After numerous visits from the social worker who was brilliant with her advice and speedy visits when needed, and trips to consultants to discuss a new medication to try, my mum's condition worsened. She was crying several times a day and started becoming anxious going out of the house. She was also upset at home because of these people that were being unkind to her. I would go round to my parent's house and take her out for lunch and she would start crying saying people were being horrible and not letting her go to the toilet. She would sometimes get up from her chair and want to leave but I usually managed to persuade her to stay. I would tell her that she was fine and if she needed a toilet she could go and I would take her. This dilemma and upset around going to the toilet happened daily. I would go to the supermarket with her and she would get anxious and say she didn't know what she was doing there and wanted to leave. It was such a difficult time for me because I wanted to help and get my mum out of the house and do things with her but every time I took her out she would get upset and uneasy and say she wanted to go home. Sometimes I didn't even make it as far as driving off the estate. She would talk to herself saying, 'your horrible you are.'

I would say, 'who's horrible?'

And she would reply, 'them in the back.'

If I questioned who was in the back she would turn around and have a look and say, 'oh they have gone now, that's what they do they just disappear.' Then she would say she wanted to go home and would make me turn the car around and drop her home. I noticed on quite a few occasions that she would talk to herself in third person if she saw herself in a mirror. She would go to the bathroom and see herself and then start saying to herself, 'your horrible you are, yes I can go to the toilet and you can't stop me.' Sometimes she would even reply back to herself like she had two personalities or an alter ego.

I remember one occasion that it happened and I'm not going to lie, it freaked me out. My mum was walking the dog with me in the woods holding a bottle of water and she started talking to herself. She was saying, 'you better drink all that drink,' 'but I don't have to drink it all why are you so horrible', 'I'm not horrible,' 'yes you are you are horrible.'

When I questioned who was horrible she said, 'her' and pointed at herself. I said what's her name and she said, 'I don't know.' When I asked what she was wearing she pointed at her own clothes and said, 'this.' She then looked angry and exclaimed, 'you don't believe me, do you?' To which I remembered what I had been told by the social worker about my mum believing what she was saying. It was all very real to her and I should agree or go along with what she was saying so that I didn't upset her.

I calmed her down and told her, 'of course I believe you, I believe you are seeing what you have seen but I can't see it otherwise I would do something about it.' My mum looked relieved that I believed her but also confused at the fact that I said I couldn't see anything. Probably something I shouldn't have said and something I have now learned to skim over in conversations and agree with the harmless untruths. On another occasion she was holding a bottle of water whilst walking the dog but this time we had my daughter with us. Millie asked nanny if she could have a drink because she was thirsty and my mum looked like she had just asked for her entire bank account. She didn't look too happy, but I said, 'it's alright if Millie has a drink, isn't it?'

And she replied, 'if she has to.' When I probed my mum why she wanted the water to herself she explained that if she didn't drink all the water herself she would be in trouble. She had to drink the water and couldn't let anybody else help her finish it. "They" would be watching and wouldn't be happy with her. As she didn't seem too distressed by what she was saying I let Millie have a quick drink and told her it would be OK, and that seemed to work.

The more upset and agitated my mum was getting with these people in her house the more often she began to wet herself. On one occasion, the first time I had physically seen her wet herself in front of me it was such a shock to my system. We again were walking the dogs in the woods, when we got about half way round and my mum just stood still. I started to see a small wet patch appear on her pale blue jeans. She looked so confused and just looked down at herself saying, 'what's happening.' The wet patch proceeded to get bigger and bigger until eventually it was right down her leg. The whole time I stood there flabbergasted at what I was witnessing and more stunned at the fact that she didn't know what was happening and also just kept saying, 'that wasn't me.'

I said, 'don't worry its fine, let's get back and get cleaned up.' The whole way home I was hoping we didn't bump into anyone in the woods because I didn't want my mum to have that humiliation of being seen with urine all down her leg. She has always been a respectful dignified lady. She was still adamant, even when we got to my house and cleaned her up, that it wasn't her that had wet the trousers. I got her washed and changed her clothes before driving her home.

I told my dad what had happened and he looked concerned because it appeared it was now happening a lot more frequently than before. My mum was so wrapped up in these people telling her she couldn't go to the toilet that it seemed obvious to us she was wetting herself because she was trying to hold herself and not go to the toilet. However, this just got worse and now we know it was just the Alzheimer's taking hold. To top it off and to make matters worse, the medication she was prescribed to help with the voices and hallucinations, reacted badly with her. She described it as feeling like she was in a tornado. She kept getting out of bed and feeling dizzy and like everything was moving around her. Then one day she was downstairs and got up from the sofa. As she stood up she lost her footing and fell into the tv that was on the tv stand. Luckily she didn't hurt herself but she was very upset and confused. She kept saying, 'why am I feeling this way, like I am in a tornado.' So she was sent to the doctors and they ran some tests. They checked her blood pressure and did an ECG. The ECG showed a small irregularity and it was decided to stop the medication. Another failed attempt at making things a bit easier or helping my mum fight this awful disease.

We continued to try and calm my mum when she got distressed at home or outside. I made every effort to try and take her out daily even if it was just to a supermarket, out for lunch, to dinner or for a walk. Even though most attempts ended in tears or she got stressed, she was still happy to go out again the following day. Every day was becoming more of a challenge and it felt like my mum's condition was getting worse by the day. Every time we got into the car she would question why I let "them" in and would shout, 'they are f***ing nasty they are!' My dad and I would try and get her to go to the toilet before going or leaving anywhere and sometimes she would sit on the toilet crying her eyes out. On occasion when she did go to the toilet she would come downstairs and say, 'I haven't been for more than one toilet today Nat, have I?' Or 'I only did a little wee, didn't I?' It's like her toilet habits were being monitored and she would get upset if she wasn't following the rules. The worst part of it all was seeing the torment and dismay in my mum's eyes when she was talking about these people and there was nothing we could do. It was so farfetched that we struggled to go along with it and she could see we were resisting what she was telling us. One day she got so upset and said that the people were being horrible and telling lies, and my face made it obvious that I didn't believe what I was being told. My mum got more upset and told me and my dad to set up a secret camera in the house so that we could see what was going on. My dad and myself exclaimed that we did believe her and that she was safe. We assured her that we didn't believe "their" lies and she could go to the toilet whenever she wanted.

The issue with the toilet went on for a few months. My mum began wetting herself much more frequently and on the odd occasion soiled herself. It became increasingly difficult to go anywhere without upset around the use of the toilet. We would go out and she would sometimes claim she had been to the toilet when actually she hadn't because she didn't flush and the water was clear with no toilet tissue down it. We knew this was because in her head she wasn't allowed to go. She would just be sat watching the television and when she stood up there would be a huge wet patch where she had wet herself. It didn't matter if her trousers were wet or if the seat was wet, she was still adamant it wasn't her that was wetting herself. When things became more difficult, I spent a lot of time around my parents. Luckily living around the corner it made it easy enough to pop in several times a day to check on them, check what needed doing and take my mum out for a walk or wherever she wanted to go. I would sometimes go out in the morning with them for a coffee, and I would usually go round to their house at lunch time to walk the dogs. I had to start going to my parent's house to walk the dogs rather than meeting my mum in the woods because more often than not she got 2 minutes up the road and ended up back at her front door. It became apparent that the simplest of journeys and tasks now had to be done with somebody because she was slowly losing her capability. Every evening I would pop round when Shaun got in from work and would take some dinner round for them both. My mum and dad have both never been great at cooking so when I was a kid meals were always quite simple and repetitive. I am far from a good cook but I have learnt to have a bit more variety now and I can make most dishes with the help of a jar or sachet. I would try and make a meal I knew my kids, husband and parents would all eat. I wanted my mum to be eating nutritious meals and I know my dad loves a cooked dinner. However it got to the point where I was taking her dinners round and she just pushed the food around the plate and didn't really eat much of it. She would much rather a bowl of cereal or toast and sweet desserts and treats. So I just started dropping meals for dad or sometimes would take a very small portion to my mum so that if it wasn't eaten, it wasn't such a waste.

On some evenings I would go round and have to shower my mum or strip the sofa because she had wet herself, or even sometimes soiled herself. On a very rare occasion I would get a call from my dad because she had soiled herself and he couldn't deal with it, so I would go round and try to help. I try my best with everything regarding my mum but one thing I cannot deny is how weak my stomach is. I remember one time I was called round and as soon as the smell hit me as I made my way to the bathroom, I was gagging so bad that I was almost sick. My dad really struggles with faeces as it reminds him of the war zones he has been in. It triggers his PTSD, so I always knew my dad wasn't going to react well to having to clean up faeces. I tried my best to help clean my mum but my dad ended up having to help me too because I just couldn't face the smell. Luckily at this stage it wasn't a regular occurrence. It was hard work but I felt like I was giving my mum the care and love she deserved whilst also helping to keep my dad's head above water and preventing him from crashing and burning. I could help my dad with everything and anything but faeces was a massive hurdle we both had to try and overcome. Although this felt like hard work this was only the very beginning of the time and effort I was going to be putting in to help with the care of my beloved mother.

In between more visits by the social worker, who we felt a very close connection with because it felt like she was on this unexpected downward rollercoaster with us from the beginning, my mum starting wetting and soiling herself a lot more. It was eventually concluded that she required some incontinence pants so that me and my dad were not forever, changing the bed, cleaning the sofa, washing clothes and showering her. The faeces had become a huge problem for my dad, he started dreading her soiling herself. He would get angry and on occasion have a go at her because the smell would instantly trigger his PTSD and if I'm being honest I don't think he had got his head around how she wasn't realising she was soiling herself when it was on her skin and in her clothes. On numerous occasions I would try and help clean my mum and if I gave her a wipe to clean herself she would not be able to co-ordinate the wipe. She would fold it the wrong way after wiping and faeces would be all over her hands and in her nails. Then the wipe would end up on the floor and she would touch something with the faeces on her hands. I could feel my patience wearing thin and although I knew it wasn't intentional, I was getting angry that she wasn't doing as I was telling her too, and I had to remind myself that getting blunt with my words or sounding slightly annoyed wasn't going to help matters. I would shower her down and faeces would be falling from her body into the shower. One element of the care that I really struggled with was the incontinence. I sometimes struggle with my baby's nappy but adult faeces is on another level. It's so hard mentally and physically to shower down and clean an adult, my mum. Not only is it hard but it's upsetting too. On numerous occasions I would be showering her with tears in my eyes because it really made me realise the extent of this disease. My dad and I tried everything to help including buying face masks and smothering the underneath of our noses with Vicks to mask the smell.

One day in particular still sticks in my mind as clear as day. I had gone round to my parents once my husband had got in from work. I walked into the house and my dad was not very happy at all, he was sat in his computer room upstairs whilst my mum was sat downstairs on the sofa. She said, 'he isn't very happy,' and went on to explain that someone had been in the bathroom and made a right mess and he was fuming. She said, 'I don't know why they did it, it was disgusting and now he's so angry with them, but I am not surprised.' She was sat in her night dress and was freshly showered so I knew something had happened and normally of an evening time my dad sat downstairs with her on the sofa and they watched tv together.

So I went upstairs to speak to my dad. When I asked what had happened and if everything was OK he explained, 'I went into the bathroom and it was like a bomb had gone off, there was poo all over the toilet, the floor, the sink and all over your mum. It was like she had intentionally spread it all over the bathroom to prove a point that somebody is doing wrong in the house.' Not only did my dad have to face that challenge of cleaning faeces up from walls and floors etc but he also had to lift my uncoordinated mum covered in faeces, over the bath so that she could be showered down. Trying to get her to stand in the bath to be showered was not only hard work physically but it was also incredibly dangerous because she was so uncoordinated and she was ten times worse when she had water in her face. Trying to use one hand to hold her steady and the other to hold the shower head and wash her down was never going to be easy. If you asked my mum to wash a certain area herself, she would sometimes struggle to follow that instruction especially when she was anxious about falling in the bath. Anxiety makes her concentration and coordination so much worse than it already is. My dad's upset at what was happening to my mum was being shown with anger and unfortunately he could not hide that from her. My dad and I are like minded and I can only imagine the thoughts running through his head whilst my mum was sat downstairs…why my wife? What happened to the few more years we had to enjoy our lives before this took hold? Why has she gone downhill so rapidly? And most importantly…What's next?

The incontinence nurse came out to have a meeting with myself, my dad and my mum. We had been using shop bought incontinence knickers and we were told to keep them for 24 hours so that they could be weighed. This would help the nurse work out what strength of pad she would need. We knew the pad she wore at night-time would be one of the higher strength pads because it was always very full in the morning and she would sometimes leak. She was prescribed heavy flow pads for night-time and light pads for the daytime, but it wasn't going to be long before she would need the heaviest flow pants all the time. When we had to start using the pads it was initially quite tricky. My mum would say, 'I'm not wearing that, I don't need to wear that.' I would always try and distract her because I learned that if I distracted her it would save her disliking me for something she felt I was doing wrong. The pads helped with daytime accidents but they were not helping with the bed wetting. We found the pads were slipping in the night and they were so full that it was still soaking the bed wet through. Between us my dad and I were changing the bedding daily and this was just a chore we didn't need on top of caring for my mum. Eventually her night-time pad was changed to a wrap around one which worked brilliantly if you could get it on. Trying to put a huge "nappy" on a large adult when they are standing up is not easy, but once on it did a good job at keeping the bed clean and dry. As the incontinence got substantially worse so did everything else. My mum would never normally say anything to upset anybody and would avoid getting into any sort of confrontation. This was all about to change.

The Accusations and Questions of Trust

As time was passing my mum slowly started separating herself from my dad and me. It was as if she started feeling like she was dealing with the "other people" herself and she was aware that nobody could see or hear what she was experiencing. This must have made her feel quite alone and like she could only trust herself. I was spending a lot of time with my mum so I was always going to see the good days, the bad days and every day in between.

It started off with relatively unharmful accusations. So if she couldn't find her second sandal she would look for a few seconds and then ask, 'Nat, have you took my sandal?' Now to me this was an absurd question. Firstly, I've never taken anything without consent from anybody and secondly why would I want one sandal? However, this was a genuine question and she really wanted to know if I had taken it. I could see the look in her eyes whilst she asked and also by her tone of voice that she meant what she said. The first time I was accused of doing wrong I didn't really know how to react because I was being accused of something I hadn't done and I was supposed to agree with what my mum believed. I also didn't want her thinking that I was doing these things that were wrong. I began to learn that I should take her more seriously when asked a question and although I didn't need to admit to a wrong doing, I could divert the question and try to explain other possible explanations. Shoes were something I was accused of taking on many occasions and also jumpers, coats or tops. Sometimes it was obvious that her accusations and thoughts stemmed from some form of truth. My mum always had so many clothes and shoes that when she was finished with them or bought new, I would have her old items. This would include her old sandals as we have the same size feet and also old dresses and jumpers. So although I would never take her old clothes or sandals without asking, it was something that we would laugh about as I always had her cast offs. This made sense as to why my mum was accusing me of taking her misplaced clothes quite often. Although initially it agitated me that I was being accused of doing wrong, I started to learn to just take it on the chin and swiftly move on.

She would even take a cardigan off in the kitchen, come into the living room and then question if I had taken her cardigan. I would tell her that she had put it in the kitchen and I would show her it so she would believe me. Then she would just laugh at me realising she had made a mistake. I think the hardest thing to get my head around was that my mum would never have accused me of these wrong doings a few years ago, because she knew I would never hurt anybody intentionally. It's like she sometimes forgot that, and although it seems trivial it hurt me a lot because it felt like she was forgetting who I was and my character.

My mum has been on some of her medications for years so it was well and truly part of her routine when she took them. She had a tablet that was taken around p.m. every night. This was a tablet that had a side effect of making her a bit more tired hence why it was given at night time. She always referred to this tablet as the one that 'knocks her out.' That wasn't its purpose but she swore by the fact that it helped her sleep. Once she became more sceptical and suspicious she started becoming reluctant to take her medication, especially the p.m. tablet. She never persevered enough that she didn't take it but she would make it obvious that she wasn't happy about it. She would accuse me and my dad of trying to get her to go to sleep and we would try and reassure her that it wasn't to make her go to sleep but she didn't believe us. She would say, 'I am not going to bed now, I'm not taking that because I don't want to go to bed.' Sometimes we would manage to persuade her that she needed to take her tablet because she always took her tablet at this time but other times we would have to give her the tablet half an hour later so that it didn't seem as early for her. When my mum became unwell I started ordering and collecting my parent's medications. I would get told by my dad when they were running low, order them, pick them up and then drop them at my parent's house. I sometimes gave my mum her medication but it was normally my dad that did it as he was with her more frequently at home. However, I remember walking the dog with her once and she was talking to herself quite a lot. I couldn't really hear what she was saying but she wasn't happy with someone or something. Then she turned to me and quite hostilely accused me of taking her medication. She said, 'you have taken my tablets haven't you.' Again in theory I should have stayed calm and tried not to agitate her by disagreeing but in reality I was annoyed that I was basically being called a thief. I told my mum quite calmly and politely considering I was upset by what she was insinuating that I did not have her tablets and that they were at home. I could see from her face she didn't believe me and I reiterated

56

that I did not have them. When it came to dealing with trivial accusations and other small issues I was learning how to deal with them on the spot. I feel I never really had much chance initially to slowly come to terms with her illness, everything that was happening was hitting me all at once and it was just one thing after the next that I had to adjust to. I was taking in a whole new way of life for my mum, trying to get used to it and this new way of life was rapidly taking over.

Not much time passed before my mum made another hurtful comment towards me, only this time my mask slipped and I couldn't pretend that it was all OK. Myself, my dad and my mum would go out most weekends. Usually a Friday or Saturday afternoon we would go into town for a bite to eat and some drinks. Once in a blue moon my sister would join us too and we would enjoy some family time together. It was apparent by now though that it was becoming less enjoyable since my mum's diagnosis and her deterioration. She would mutter to herself, she would get upset numerous times and I would spend half my time in the toilet with her, not actually able to enjoy my free time with my parents and away from the children for a few hours. She would sit looking upset so I would say, 'do you need a toilet.'

To which she would normally respond with, 'yes I've been needing a toilet for ages but I haven't been allowed to go,' or 'no I don't need one,' even though it was very obvious she needed a toilet. If she did go to the toilet I would go with her and sometimes I could be stood outside her cubicle for about 10 minutes. To make matters worse she would come out of the cubicle and when asked if she had been she would either say yes but the toilet was empty and it hadn't been flushed or she would say no because she wasn't allowed to go. Sometimes she would be adamant that she wanted to get out of the toilet so I would take her back to the table, for me to have to take her back to the toilet 5 minutes later. The more liquids she drank the more frequently she needed a toilet and not once was it as simple as it should have been. It never felt like I was out with my mum it constantly felt like me, her and this third person (the horrible one). I was battling against some sort of hidden evil force that was preventing my mum from enjoying herself like she once did. I was spending time away from my children to have some peace and quiet and enjoy myself but would finish the evening more stressed than when I went out. Not one weekend went by that I didn't go out with my parent's though if they wanted to go out. Even though it was tough I knew my dad needed my help and support and I wanted my mum to continue a normal life as much as she possibly could.

One afternoon my dad, his neighbour, my mum, my sister and myself had gone out for food and drinks. We hadn't been out long when you could see my mum wasn't in the best of moods. If she wasn't muttering to herself she was saying nothing. There was always a bit of an atmosphere when all of us went out once her illness got worse because we were waiting for her to either kick off or get upset. For myself and my dad it was like we were holding on to hope that we could continue to enjoy something we had done for a long while. However, we both knew deep down it was harder work and not so pleasurable anymore, and also anything could happen. About 20 minutes in and we had just got our first drink, and my mum was getting annoyed about something. My sister took her to the toilet, which was a nice break for me from doing the toilet runs every single time. After quite a long while they headed back to the table. I read into things quite a lot and I also pull apart a situation to work out the how, why and when. When my mum went to sit down, she made it very apparent she didn't want to sit down next to me. She swapped over next to my sister and wouldn't look at me. I took this with a pinch of salt initially because I was fully aware of her change in personality sometimes and had dealt with accusations previously so I thought she would just snap out of it. However, after a few more minutes of awkwardness my sister turned to me and told me quietly that my mum had said something horrible about me. Now if I could turn back the clock and not find out what she said then I would but it's very difficult to be told something was said and not actually find out what. Its human nature to be inquisitive when you are given some but not all information. I said I wanted to know what was said and that was when I heard the words I never wanted to hear my mum say about me, she had said that she HATED me. My eyes misted over and my heart broke as I tried to keep up appearances. I sat there broken and horrified by what I had heard for a few more minutes until eventually the emotion took over and I got up without saying anything and walked out of the pub. I stood outside the pub sobbing my heart out because as selfish and naïve as it sounds I felt like I didn't deserve to be hated by the lady that I did everything in my power to make happy and gave a huge amount of my time to. I knew it was the Alzheimer's and not my mum talking and I had been expecting her to say something hurtful to me one day, but I just couldn't react the way I had told myself I would. I was so upset and I think her cold actions towards me were playing a part in my anguish. I can't actually put into words how upset I was. I felt distraught that she had said what she had but I felt so angry at the Alzheimer's for making my mum into a person that would say something like that to me. It would have been easier if I could have been angry with her but I couldn't, because I knew it wasn't her fault.

Not long after I had walked out, my sister came outside. I don't think she realised that what she told me was going to make me react the way I did but she must have known it would upset me. I am very emotional and don't deal well with being hurt very well. I'd rather be punched in the face any day because I can deal with that sort of pain a lot easier. I rarely get angry or aggressive I just cry. Some people describe themselves as being thick skinned whereas I am the complete opposite to this. My sister said not to worry about it and that it wasn't mum saying it. She went on to say, that we were all hated, distrusted or being accused of things from one day to the next so I shouldn't take it to heart. I knew what she was saying was true but what I couldn't seem to express was that although I knew it wasn't her, it was still upsetting. I felt like I just needed time to have a cry and be upset and then I would get over it. Hearing your mum has said she hates you for the first time ever, ill or not, isn't nice. It's something I felt I needed to get my head around and if that meant crying and getting upset then so be it. I wasn't going to hold a grudge but I'm also not very good at pretending I am OK when I'm not. In between uncontrollable sobbing I told my sister I just couldn't stop being upset and I just wanted to go home. There was no way I could go back into that pub and sit down and act like nothing had happened. I was so wounded by what I knew that I needed time to process what was happening. I also couldn't help but be slightly disappointed that my sister told me what had been said. At such a rough time with my mum and knowing how emotional I was I felt it was information that should have been kept from me for my own good. I didn't really need to know because it was just going to hurt me and at this moment in time I was pretty fragile anyway with all the emotions I was facing. Maybe if my sister realised the extent of my connection with my mum and the amount of time and effort I was putting in daily without fail then she would have thought twice about pushing me a little bit nearer to the black hole I felt like I was falling in. There have been numerous occasions that my mum had made hurtful comments about my sister and this was previous to her diagnosis and after, in fact it was a regular occurrence, and still happens now. Before the diagnosis some of the comments my mum made were very harsh but I just brushed them off and would have never repeated what was said to my sister, because it would have not had a positive effect telling her. I used to think why is my mum being so critical and unforgiving with her words but now I realise it was the Alzheimer's rearing its ugly head.

That late afternoon I could not go back into the pub, so my sister went back inside to inform my dad that I was going home. A few minutes later my dad came outside to see me. He seemed to be a bit annoyed that I was upset over something my mum didn't mean. He told me that she was going to say things about us all and we had to come to terms with the fact that my mum had a disease that will change who she is and we can't get upset every time she's offensive or rude. He said we needed to take it on the chin and not let it offend us. I could see my dad was upset that I was obviously so distraught and I got what he meant but I did explain that I couldn't help feeling hurt and upset. The only way I could describe the upset is, if somebody offered me £20,000 to go back in that pub and be OK and stop crying, I couldn't have no matter how hard I tried. The tears just kept coming and coming and I couldn't stop. I said I just needed to deal with it by going home and then moving on from what had happened. He wanted me to stay but I think this shows that he didn't realise how hurt I was. I was so distraught that it was best for everyone I went home so that I could control my emotions and start a new day. I told my dad I would book him a taxi for when he was ready to leave and my sister decided she was going to share a taxi home with me. He went back inside but not before giving me a hug which made me cry a little bit more. If I get a hug I must really need it because I don't do affection. Our taxi arrived and we jumped in and made our way home. Those words, 'mum said she hates you,' went over and over in my head. I snivelled the whole way home and when I walked through my front door, I broke down explaining to my husband what had happened. Anybody else could tell me they hate me but not my mum, anybody but my mum. I went to bed distraught that night but knew in the grand scheme of things this was only a snippet of the heart break I was going to experience in the coming months.

A Break in The Chain of Routine

My mum and dad had always had a very routine day. They would get up go to Costa together and some mornings I would go along with them to. They would have their breakfast and maybe pop into a shop or two and then go home. My mum would walk the dog, they would chill into the afternoon and I would take her out if I was going out anywhere. Most afternoons I would take her somewhere just to get her out for an hour, but the days were generally the same and had been for years before. However, this routine was going to be broken with my dad having a planned trip to London coming up. Initially my dad should have been going with my mum but with her deterioration and her love of being at home we just knew this wasn't possible without help. So I suggested to my dad that he had some time away from everything that had been happening by taking my husband Shaun along with him instead. I assured my dad that between myself and my sister we could look after our mum and make sure she was OK until he got back. We knew it would be a challenge but also thought it would be OK because she was so use to me being around anyway.

When my mum's Alzheimer's started deteriorating I spent several evenings a week round my dad's sitting with her whilst he went to the gym. Initially she was left on her own but she would be upset when he got back or hiding in a room, so we knew she needed someone with her at all times. Most of the time my mum just sat down with a cup of tea and chatted or watched tv and then it became a bit more difficult. She would pace the floor or she would say she was going out soon. She went upstairs and started pulling all her clothes out the wardrobe because she needed to get ready for when my dad got home because they were going out (they were not going anywhere but my mum believed otherwise). Sometimes she would wait at the front door for my dad to come home but she never wandered off, I always managed and she was always safe. So although I knew it would be difficult and challenging I also thought that my dad deserved the break and my mum wouldn't be too much trouble without my dad's presence.

I dropped my dad at the train station with Shaun and told them both to have a good time. For my dad it was a break from caring for a few days and for Shaun it was a break from working and being a house husband whilst I cared for my parent's the minute he walked through the door from work. My dad said to me that he didn't want me to contact him regarding my mum he wanted me to just get on with it. I knew by this he meant he didn't need to hear about all the little struggles because he would worry and wouldn't be able to enjoy himself. He didn't need to know that she had soiled the bed, or wet the sofa, or accused us of wrong doings etc. I told him I would not ring, and I am a woman of my word.

Once they had been dropped at the station the plan was for me to have mine and my sister's children at my house and then she could stay at my mum's house with her and stay with her overnight. I couldn't stay overnight because Charlotte needed her cot and her bedtime routine. I explained to my sister that I would sort the kids in the morning and I would come straight over to the house and then we would share the care and take our mum out for a coffee like my dad would normally do. It was only a few hours after my dad had left, my sister was with my mum and I took all the kids to mine. My sister said she was going to order a Chinese for them both, but what should have been a nice mother and daughter night in soon turned sour pretty quickly and I got a call off my sister. She explained that my mum was wanting to get out of the house and didn't want to stay in. Normally I would go straight round but with Shaun being away it would have meant taking all the children too and this just wasn't something I wanted to do if I didn't need to. If my mum was anxious, upset or a little bit higher rate than normal then the last thing any of us needed was five children adding to the mix. I told my sister that she just needed to try calm her down and pre occupy her because I couldn't really come round with the kids. I told her not to worry because it was normal for my mum to be a little bit more active pacing the floor when my dad went out or for her to talk to herself more often than normal. It was hard for me because I wished I could be there. My mum spends pretty much every day with me and I think I understand her and can see what's going to happen next. I have been there with the Alzheimer's from the start and through every stage so I had a better understanding than my sister. I have been through every single event, appointment, tear, laughter, episode, and battle and this has made me not only closer with my mum but it's made me be able to see when somethings wrong and how she is feeling without her telling me. I've learned to be able to deal with her a lot easier and more smoothly. I also think my mum would have been more comfortable with my presence as it wasn't normal for her to spend time with my sister on her own. My sister hung up the phone and said she would ring me if things got worse.

A few minutes later I got another phone call. This time things had escalated and my sister explained how my mum was trying to push her out of the way. This was really out of character for my mum, although she had been saying things that were out of character she had never been physical in anyway. I told my sister that I would ring my parents long-time friend and neighbour Elaine. She has known my mum for many years and has always made it known that she's there if I need her or if I need help. I hung up the phone to my sister and told her I would ring her back. I phoned Elaine and explained the situation and she said she would go over, so I rung my sister back and told her that Elaine would pop over to help and to keep me updated. A while later I got a call from my sister explaining what was happening. My mum had settled down and was eating Chinese before going to bed, however it wasn't without a battle to get her to relax and sit down. My sister described how when Elaine got round my mum was still adamant she was going out even though it was dark. Elaine tried to explain to her that it was cold and dark and that she should sit down, relax and have a cup of tea. Initially my mum was having none of it and was trying to forcefully get out of the front door. She was pushing and also tried to hit her way out of the house. She punched the wall and was acting very aggressively and agitated. Elaine eventually managed to calm my mum down and got her sitting down with a cup of tea. After some time it seemed she wasn't in that agitated state anymore so Elaine left and said to call if she was needed. After hearing all that I was shocked. I never thought my mum would react to anything in that manner because she had never shown that sort of anger or aggression before. Was this really a reaction to the break in routine? My dad wasn't there like he always was and although she never asked, was she upset at his absence? We thought we had dealt with the worst of it and only had another whole day and night to go, but this was only the beginning and the next day was going to be a whole lot worse.

The next morning I got all the kids sorted and dropped off to the relevant schools, and I met my sister back at my mum's house at about 9a.m. I was informed that my mum had stayed dry and didn't soil herself in the night which was a relief to my sister. However, she then went on to add that my mum was acting quite agitated again. We wanted to try and keep to some sort of routine so we asked her if she wanted to go to Costa for breakfast and she agreed but was getting increasingly restless by the minute. She was talking to herself all the time and was talking about the fact she was going away on holiday and she had to meet someone to get a taxi to meet her husband.

Within ten minutes of my arrival my mum had gone from looking agitated to looking and sounding like she had lost all sense of reality. She started walking up and down the court where she lived heading towards the main road each time. One of us followed her and tried to encourage her to go inside but she was adamant she was waiting for her taxi. She started saying things like, 'I don't need my coat because my husband's rich and he will get me a new one, I have got to

64

wait for the taxi to take me to meet my husband because he's waiting for me,' and 'did you not know that my husband was rich, he's a millionaire he's got loads of money.' She wasn't making any sense but I just listened and acknowledged what she was saying. I rang my friend Serena and she said she would come over for support. She is a paramedic and I knew she would be cool, calm and collected and also give me the advice I needed. It was a cold wet day and not the sort of weather you would want to stand in unless you had to. We got our mum a coat but she kept walking in the house for two minutes and taking it off and then going back outside without it. When told to put her coat on she would reply, 'I don't need it because my husband will get me all new stuff when I get there.' My sister and I just thought that maybe my dad's absence had hit her harder than we thought but she would soon come back in the house and chill out.

My friend Serena had arrived and was quite taken aback by what she was witnessing, my mum was normally more with reality. We were still walking up and down the court, and sometimes she was walking further up the path along the road towards the exit of the estate. By this time my mum had gone from walking casually up and down to getting quite frantic. She was pacing so quickly she began to look red faced, sweaty and unwell. She was doing more exercise now than she had in her entire life and she also hadn't eaten and wasn't drinking. She had gone from taxi to helicopter and was asking me if I could see the helicopter. There were no helicopters in sight but my mum was adamant a helicopter was going to pick her up and she was number 11 and numbers 1-10 were being picked up first. She explained to me how the helicopter 'whipped them up into the air' and asked me if I saw the line come down and whip them up into the helicopter. I explained I couldn't see it. She was pacing up and down, up and down shouting out numbers like she was calling them to their positions. It was like a live action film occurring right in front of me but I had to use my imagination as I couldn't see most of the film happening. When she got towards the front door of the house we were trying to coax her into the house and telling her to come and get a nice cup of tea but she refused. She started yelling at us to move our cars, my car was parked in front of her house. She was saying I needed to move it now or she would crush it. She explained that the helicopter couldn't get to the house because my car was in the way. She came right up to my face and pointed her finger at me shouting to move my car. She almost sounded like she was going to cry because it was that important to her.

We managed to get her in the house for about twenty minutes but she was restless and after that time she headed straight to the front door. My sister tried to prevent her by locking the door and she got really upset and irritated getting in our faces and shoving us. At one point she went to punch my sister and she punched the stairs instead. My sister isn't as easily intimidated as myself and I was quite scared that my mum would attack one of us because there was no way I would hurt her back by defending myself. She was shouting in my face and the look of hatred in her face when she stared me cold in the eyes was very apparent. She wasn't going to give up and she was getting more and more troubled which in turn was leading to aggression. I decided it was best the door was unlocked and she was allowed out. I could understand our thought process in locking the door because it was for her own safety but I also could see and understand the upset locking my mum inside her own house was causing. She has never liked being locked in anywhere and is very claustrophobic so what else did we expect? She headed back out the house with no shoes on her feet, on the cold wet concrete. She was too busy shouting to these "other people" to listen to any advice given to her. She started shouting abuse about the cars again and then carried on her mission, pacing back and forth waiting for some form of transport. I offered her a drink as she was looking increasingly unwell and she refused saying I had probably poisoned it. I turned and said to my sister, 'something has to be done because this isn't right and we cannot spend all day walking the streets with mum. She looks unwell and there's no sign of improvement.' Serena also agreed my mum needed help, advised me to call the social worker and then had to get back home.

I made the tough decision to involve the social worker by giving her a call but first I needed to inform my dad and make sure I was making the right decision. Although my dad told me to not ring him and not to bug him I felt this was not your general day to day problem and he needed to know what was happening. So I went out of ear shot of my mum and rang my dad. I explained the situation through tears and he told me to do what needed doing. I think he realised that she needed help. I told him not to worry and that I would sort it. I then rang the social worker who I think may have been expecting some sort of breakdown with my dad not being there. She told me she would come out and that she would be about an hour. I think she also knew from my call that things were bad because she never saw me get emotional unless there's something really wrong. My mum had now been pacing the roads and streets for several hours. My back was aching, my feet hurting, my head pounding and my stomach shouting at me for not eating anything that day so far. I was getting quite concerned about her and her lack of food and drink whilst exerting herself.

After a little longer than expected, the social worker arrived with her assistant. I think they were quite gobsmacked by the change in my mum. She was telling them to go away and that she wasn't crazy, answering them back and refusing to co-operate when asked to put a coat and shoes on. She laughed at them like they were mad when they asked why she was outside and she explained. Everything was so real to her and this crazy world she was in right now with the helicopters and planes, taxis, and her rich husband was very real. The only way I could get her to put her coat on was to tell her that her husband said she needed to put it on, then she agreed to it. At one point my mum was leaking urine down her leg so she eventually went inside. She went upstairs to change herself and came down with no trousers or knickers on. She tried to come outside until she was stopped and told she needed something on. She tried to resist the request but eventually listened and put some trousers on backwards. The social worker explained to me that my mum was very unwell and needed help and that she would unfortunately need to be sectioned. It was very strange how I was feeling at this point because I wasn't feeling huge upset right now. I think the adrenalin was pumping and I didn't have the time to feel upset in between managing my then 7-month-old, following my mum up and down the street, and talking through things with the social worker. It was nonstop and I didn't have much time to take anything in. I felt concerned, confused and shocked but I wasn't crying which was unlike me.

After a while two health professionals showed up and it was very apparent that the section was being put into motion for my mum. They couldn't have a conversation with her, she just kept saying I'm not mad. She couldn't say anything or do anything to prove she was in our reality and she was making no sense. It was making me upset but more angry that it had to come to her being sectioned, but if that's what the professionals say then that must be what's best for my mum? Wasn't it? So I let them take control of the situation whilst trying to reassure my mum everything was OK. The third professional, the AMHP eventually showed up and they all agreed officially my mum needed sectioning. They said we would need to wait for an ambulance to the hospital, and that she would be going to a hospital about a 30-minute drive away. It was rung through and we were given a waiting time of a couple of hours. We now had to hope that my mum would go nicely into the ambulance because if she didn't it was explained to us that she would have to have police assistance and they would be able to use some force to get her onto the ambulance and that is not what I wanted to see. I explained to my mum that an ambulance would be coming soon and they needed to take her to help with her medication. She was instantly against the idea and said, 'I am not going anywhere I don't need an ambulance.' I just hoped I could persuade her otherwise when the ambulance got there.

After more than a few hours everybody was getting restless including myself. It seemed that my mum was a very low priority call to the emergency services. My sister and I took it upon ourselves to ring for an ambulance and explain that my mum had Alzheimer's and was looking pale and sweaty and clenching her chest at times. I told my sister to make the call because we may have slightly exaggerated the chest pain to get their attention. I would have been a stuttering mess because I hate lying but to be honest we didn't know how my mum was feeling and she didn't have the mental capacity to describe any issues. She looked pale and sweaty and was very distressed and we honestly felt she was going to collapse any minute because she just would not stop. We got told an ambulance would be on its way and not too long after we received a paramedic.

My mum got checked over and our minds were put at rest as her checks all came back OK, however we still had to wait for an ambulance as the paramedic was in a car. Also somewhere along the communications the police arrived and they went over to my mum to speak with her. However, they didn't stay long and just said that if we needed them to call back and say we needed their assistance. They could see that although she wasn't well she wasn't causing any problems that required police assistance just yet.

The social worker and her assistant soon left as there wasn't much more they could do but their help that day was amazing. They helped us with my mum, following her up the street, trying to keep as much of her dignity as possible, they helped with my baby, they even went as far as bottle feeding her whilst I was following my mum and trying to keep her busy by talking to her. Without their help that day I think I would have reached breaking point. They even waited with my mum whilst we went to pick our kids up from school. Elaine then took mine and my sister's children to her house round the corner whilst we waited for the ambulance as it wasn't something we wanted the kids to see.

The ambulance soon arrived and the paramedics introduced themselves to my mum. They explained why they were there and they were very friendly and understanding with her. I packed a few things into a bag whilst they did some basic checks. I could see the look of confusion, disbelief and fury on my mum's face that she had an ambulance waiting for her as she was adamant she didn't need to go anywhere and she 'wasn't mad.' I kept trying to explain to her that she just needed to go with them to have some help with her medication but she was refusing. I clarified to her that if she didn't go she would be forced to go so it would be best all round if she went off her own accord. She wasn't happy but with some persuasion and me by her side she headed towards the ambulance. I just hoped she would take those last few steps into the ambulance. I was so relieved when she walked with me and didn't hold back because there was no way I was going to physically force my mum anywhere and it would have been very disturbing for me to see her forced by police. We walked to the entrance of the ambulance and as we got there my mum said no and pulled back slightly. I explained again that she needed to go and that everything would be OK. She took a step onto the ambulance but then didn't take the second step. She was so reluctant that she didn't make the effort to lift up onto the second step. It was quite a large steep step but I think her conscious was purposely making it more difficult for her to get up because she didn't want to go. So with the paramedics help and myself pushing from behind we got her onto the ambulance. When she got onto the ambulance she started crying, she said she didn't want to go and was really distressed. This was such a heart-breaking moment for me. Not only is my mum really claustrophobic and she's being put onto the back of a closed in ambulance but she also never goes anywhere on her own. She always had myself or my dad with her, and she was like this way before the Alzheimer's. She also doesn't like change or not knowing what's happening. I know if I was in her shoes, being taken to an unknown place on my own I would have been anxious and scared. I gave her a kiss and said goodbye and even though she was pleading with me and crying, I knew there was nothing I could do so I just walked away. I cried my heart out as soon as my back was turned. Once the ambulance started driving away I felt a sense of guilt. Had I done the right thing? My mum has Alzheimer's she isn't mentally unstable. Have I just made things worse? Is she going to cope with this change? But I also thought about what would have happened if she wasn't sectioned. Could we have coped much longer? All I knew right now was that my children needed picking up and I needed to get home. I was emotionally and physically drained, it had been a long 9-hour day and I needed some time to process what had just happened.

The next day I felt like I had drunk a bottle of spirits and then dragged through a hedge backwards. My head was pounding and my body was aching. I was so shocked at what had happened and still upset with my decision to have my mum taken away. It was really distressing to think of her sat in some hospital somewhere and not having a clue where she was or what she was doing there. She would be surrounded by unfamiliar faces and away from her home. I rang the hospital and asked how she was, they told me she was quite unsettled and wasn't really eating but she was OK. This upset me more and I asked their advice about visiting and they recommended I left it a few days so that my mum could settle in. I then spoke to the social worker who also advised I let her settle before visiting. So I took the advice given and avoided going to see her for a few days. When my dad arrived home from London on the Friday he was in shock I think. He couldn't believe a few days away ended up with him coming home to an empty house. He was upset but also relieved that this all happened whilst he wasn't there so he didn't need to see my mum go through it all. She went into the hospital on Thursday early evening and we had a party coming up on the Saturday in Manchester. It was my nanas 80th birthday, my dad's mum. We were in two minds whether to go or whether we should leave it, however family were really looking forward to seeing us and my nana wouldn't be having another 80th birthday party ever again. My dad decided that after speaking with relatives that we would still go to the party on the Saturday and then come home on the Sunday. As we couldn't do anything to help my mum and couldn't see her, there wasn't much use in staying at home.

Going to the party without my mum was really strange, however it was lovely seeing everyone and the party was brilliant. It was perfectly organised and real fun but was so bizarre without my mum to sit with or talk to. I had a drink, some food, a dance and the kids loved it, however once the alcohol kicked in so did reality. Being at a family event without her was like dancing to no music or watching a film with an eye mask on. It just wasn't right and it felt like something was missing. Watching my dad walk around talking to people on his own and not having my mum by his side where she belonged, was hard to see. It got a bit much towards the end and my sister and I shed a few tears. I really enjoyed my evening but it would have been so much better if she could have been there. It went through my head a few times that we were having fun and laughing and dancing whilst she was sat in some hospital probably deteriorating. My mum was out of sight but she most definitely was not out of mind.

Once we got home the next day I said to my dad that I wanted to go and see my mum in the hospital and see how she was. He said it wasn't a good idea but on this occasion I wasn't going to listen because she was my mum and I needed to know that she was OK. I couldn't bear the thought of leaving her on her own without some reassurance from someone that things would be alright. My dad decided he would come with me so that he could drive me there but he said he would wait in the car, as he didn't want to get upset and I think he needed me to tell him what it was like first before he saw something that could not be unseen.

Mental Health Hospital 1 Added Accusations, Anxiety, Anger and Absent Belongings

After about half an hour drive me and my dad arrived outside the hospital my mum was in. I got out of the car and nervously walked towards a door that had a buzzer on the outside, whilst my dad stayed in the car. I pressed the buzzer and said I was there to see Susan Yarwood and somebody said they would be down to let me in shortly. A few minutes later a member of staff came to the door and let me in. Straight away I was uneasy because no hospital is a great place to be in but a mental health hospital or dementia unit is a bit more daunting as you don't know what to expect when you walk in at all. As I walked through a few locked doors and down some corridors I was shown to a large communal room. It was dull, and not very exciting. Just loads of chairs all going round a huge room and a tv in the corner. The first few people I saw were very old, one was asleep dribbling in a chair and the other was trying to get up from her chair. I was so shocked and upset by what I was viewing because I just never imagined it would be like this. My initial thoughts straight away were, what have I done? There were so many Zimmer frames in front of me, it was like I was in an old people's home. I turned my head further round and saw more very old people all asleep, and then I saw my mum. She was sat in a chair talking to herself, I know it's probably not the best phrase to use but she looked mental. Her clothes were on incorrectly, her hair a mess, and she was talking and laughing to herself. I walked over to her and was really apprehensive about the greeting I would get. Would she remember that I got her put into this hospital? Would she forgive me? Have I made her hate me? When she saw me she smiled and said, 'alright Nat.' I asked if she was OK and she said she was. However, she then started talking about the most random topics and nothing she said made any sense. She spoke about how she was going on holiday the next day and she needed to get packed. She spoke about her dog Lulu and explained how she was worried about her, and spoke about how she had been outside and then been to the shops that day. When I think about that day it wasn't really her talking she was rambling, each sentenced rolled into the next. It was a worrying sight for me as it was like she wasn't aware of expressing how she felt but she was obviously highly anxious and on edge. At one point she made a passing comment about the day she was sectioned but made no reference to myself. She did mention my sister and said, 'she got me taken like I was mental and I am not.'

I asked, 'who me?'

And she said, 'No Dan,' and that was followed with a few explicit words. I informed my mum that she needed some help with medication and that was why myself and my sister decided she needed to go and see a doctor to help. She didn't really acknowledge my reply and then continued to ramble about a different topic. I found it strange how she didn't acknowledge I was there the day she was sectioned as I was the one who put her on the ambulance, but I suppose that's Alzheimer's for you. Some moments, days and years are cemented into the brain and others just disappear like they never even happened.

There were a couple of members of staff about and I thought it best I speak to them about what was going to happen with my mum as my gut feeling and my heart was telling me this was not the best place for her. It's like she had lost more of herself whilst she had been in there and she was getting more and more confused and anxious about what was happening as time went on. She spoke about my dad several times whilst I was there, saying they were going away and he was going to come and find her. It was the one thing that kept me from breaking down in tears there and then, seeing the unbreakable connection my mum had with my dad. Still being able to see the love she held for him and that he was always in her thoughts, even now. After a long chat with my mum I said goodbye through tear filled eyes and explained I would be back soon. She looked upset and I think the only reason she didn't break down crying was because she believed my dad was coming to take her on holiday and if that was making her happy then I was glad she had those fictional beliefs. I went to speak to one of the senior members of staff to find out what was happening and how my mum really was. She explained to me that my mum could be kept in the hospital for a number of weeks and that they would try and find a medication to help her with the voices and hallucinations etc. I asked what would happen if I thought it wasn't the right place for her and she told me that I could appeal the section and informed me how I would do that. The staff member explained that my mum was

74

eating now and seemed to be more settled but to me these precious moments of her life with Alzheimer's should not be spent in a hospital where she had no fresh air, nothing to do, and everybody was elderly and sleeping with Zimmer frames. It was no disrespect to the other people but my mum was still quite mobile and she had very limited space to walk around. The facilities were very confined with lots of locked doors and no windows. I felt like my she was being punished for having Alzheimer's and treated like a mental patient rather than being cared for. She had been put through enough when she was given this soul fading, life destroying diagnosis.

I was directed out of the building and I felt an overwhelming sense of guilt for allowing my mum to be placed in somewhere like that. I just kept thinking she should have been at home on her chair in the living room watching tv with a biscuit and a cup of tea. I would never ever forget that image of her sat in that chair in a room filled with elderly people not getting the love and attention she got whilst at home. No hot chocolate before bed, no footstool for her feet to be rested on whilst watching tv and no big double bed for her to sprawl out on. I stepped outside after shedding a few tears to myself and got back into the car with my dad. He asked me what my mum was like and what the place was like. I really tried to fight back my emotions before I told him and I was adamant I wasn't going to cry. I took a few gulps to make sure I was fully prepared to talk but as soon as I started talking I could feel my lips starting to quiver and my eyes filling up again. Sometimes I think the harder I try not to cry the worse I actually cry and I just burst into tears. I explained that I felt my mum didn't deserve to be in there and that she was surrounded by old people all sleeping. It was very dull, boring and more like a very old residential building. It was not what I imagined for my mum and I believed she would be somewhere warm and caring, not locked in a mental institution being left to deteriorate further. After telling my dad everything I could sense his upset and between us we decided we would be getting her out of there as quickly as possible. However we had no idea how difficult getting her out of a section was going to be and how much worse the next few days were going to get whilst she was in hospital.

The next day I rang the hospital and asked about my mum, they again reassured me that she was much more settled. However after seeing that she was happy enough to see me the previous day there was no way I wasn't going to visit my her again. I needed her to know she wasn't on her own and hadn't been abandoned. I also rang the social worker and asked about how I would go about getting my mum out of the hospital and back home. She told me that I needed to leave it for a while because she needed help with her medication and she was in the best place. She said that my mum had been sectioned and that meant rules and processes needed to be followed but she was in the right place for now. I was gutted but at the same time it made me think that hopefully something could be sorted to help her so we never had an episode like we did that day again. So that evening when Shaun got in from work my dad and I went to see my mum again. I thought it couldn't be any more emotional than the first visit but how wrong was I. As we walked in and turned a few corners we could see down the end of a long corridor. My mum was at the other end of the corridor and my dad whistled and called her, she turned around and her eyes lit up. She ran down the corridor and wrapped her arms around my dad and began to cry telling him how much she had missed him. That was really hard to see because it felt cruel that she was in the hospital and not with the man that kept her heart glowing. We were shown to a family room so that we could have some privacy and whilst we walked the few steps to the room my mum was clinging onto my dad like a baby monkey clings to its mother. She was obviously very happy to see my dad but I was also apprehensive about the fact we would have to leave her there in a short while. She wasn't going to be letting go of my dad easily. We sat down and my dad got us all a drink. I had chocolates for my mum so she sat down and started eating her way through them saying she was hungry. She was very nervous and obviously confused about what was happening. She was talking to us but was talking so quick it was hard to understand everything she was saying. However one thing myself and my dad did notice was that she was talking differently, every sentence was finished with a Manchester accent. We had a laugh about it because she is originally from Manchester but hasn't lived there for years, and apart from a few words she doesn't normally sound like she is from there. She sounded so different, it was bizarre.

My mum was also saying very strange and unusual things about the staff and how they were behaving. She was getting very disturbed and dismayed saying they were locking her in a cupboard and not letting her eat or drink. She even went as far to say that he was fiddling with the girls whilst they were sleeping, but they were not going to do it to her because she would kick them in the balls. This sort of language and sexual conversation was so unlike her, so it made it even more weird to hear. At one point a male member of staff came into the family room to check we were OK and my mum accused him of trying to sleep

76

with her. The guy looked slightly embarrassed as she was accusing him in front of us and she was looking at him like a piece of dirt. If it wasn't for the guy being gay, as he explained his husband wouldn't have appreciated him doing that, I may have been slightly concerned but I was more embarrassed for the poor man. Myself and my dad sort of lightly laughed it off and then tried to divert my mum's attention. She continued to tell us how they were horrible and beat them with sticks and she had to hide because she was scared. She described how on one occasion she had to hide under the desk because he was looking for the woman and getting in their beds whilst they slept. The woman had diseases because they had slept with the men. I had no idea why my mum had these thoughts but it was quite apparent they were untrue. After about an hour of her clinging to my dad and getting upset about what she believed was going on, it was time for us to say goodbye. We all walked together back to the corridor and then we had to leave her. My dad gave her a kiss and said goodbye and explained that we would be back, but she was extremely distressed by this. She was holding with such a firm grip to my dad that a member of staff had to help prise my mum off and tell her it would be OK. She started crying and walked off in the opposite direction like she was looking for a way out. As we walked down the corridor towards a door we could still hear her crying and it was so heart-breaking. My dad saw the room with all the elderly in the chairs and could see that my mum was not in somewhere we would want for her. The fact that she wanted to come home to be with him just broke every single one of his heart strings and he was so frustrated he gently punched the wall and broke down in tears. He angrily exclaimed, 'do not bring me here again, I can't do this!' I could see that he was utterly broken and was talking through frustration and upset. I got tearful because I just wanted my mum and dad to be happy and seeing her changing into somebody I didn't know was killing me but seeing my dad fight back tears was killing me twice over.

Over the next few days I went every single day to see my mum. Had a chat with her, took her treats, even took the kids one evening to make things appear more normal to her. My dad didn't mean what he said because after a day or two he came back to the hospital one evening with me. We went back into the family room again and my mum still had her Manchester accent and was still accusing the staff of everything and anything. Whilst sat down we noticed her breath was really bad like her teeth were not getting brushed, and her trousers were on backwards. My dad then also spotted one of her rings was missing from her finger. It was her eternity ring that he had purchased for her a few years ago. He wasn't very happy as he felt that although she was in a hospital, she should have been having her teeth brushed and her clothes put on correctly. My mum needed assistance to complete these basic tasks and the staff should have realised that. If she was at home, she would have been getting all the care and more from us and it was upsetting to see that her care was lacking. We went to her room and had a quick look for the ring, under the bed, in the draws and on the floor but the ring was nowhere to be seen. We also noticed her electric toothbrush was rock hard and obviously hadn't been used. My dad is very hygienic and also believes basic human hygiene should never be forgotten so he was not best pleased. He found somebody in charge and explained about my mum's ring and his concern for its whereabouts. The staff member said they would look around and make sure people kept their eyes open for it. So after feeling frustrated and annoyed my dad decided it best we leave. So we said our hard goodbyes and left.

As if one ring wasn't enough, when we went back the following day one of my mum's other rings was now missing from another finger. It was my mum's grandma's wedding band so not of great worth, but very sentimental. My dad was fuming and decided to track down a member of staff again. They went to have a look in the inventory that was recorded when my mum was booked in to see what belongings they had noted down. They had 3 rings recorded and booked in but she actually had 4 rings. This straight away wasn't a great start because they hadn't even done that job properly and then they just said they would look for the rings but didn't offer any understanding words or try to make us feel any better about what had happened. They just blamed my mum and said she had probably taken them off. My dad's anger always takes full force in situations like this whereas I was fully aware that my she could have probably taken the rings off and left them somewhere. However that wasn't for definite and I expected a bit more understanding and help from the staff rather than brushing it off like it was nothing. We left that day even more frustrated and angry and more determined that my mum wasn't staying much longer in there. She was going home where she could be cared for properly.

I spoke to the social worker again and explained that we did not want my mum in that hospital anymore and described the situation. She was very understanding and said she would speak to the consultant dealing with her and would get back to me. A few hours later she informed me that my mum could not just be let out but that they would do a review on the Friday and that could possibly result in my mum being allowed home. She said a review will give everybody the chance to talk and see where we would go from there. We had a few days to wait but we knew there wasn't anything else that could be done, so I just continued to visit my mum and just hoped time would pass by quickly for her sake.

The Review

A few days before the review myself and my dad had time to think, reflect and prepare for what we were going to say to help get my mum home. Between us we decided that it was probably best my dad gave the gym up if he needed to. My dad had been a member of the gym for as long as I can remember and his fitness is very important to him and his mental health. However, he knew that if going out for a few hours was going to cause my mum to have a downward spiral then he needed to be at home for her as much as possible. It wasn't a decision that he made easily as he knew that his time to chill, reflect and have some respite was going to be dramatically reduced. He decided he was going to get an exercise bike and would do his fitness at home. If this didn't prove to the professionals in that review that we were both serious and would do whatever it took to have her home then what would. We were going to go into that review and speak from the heart and do what we could to get the outcome we wanted.

The day finally came and my stomach was in knots. I didn't know what to expect and didn't know what the outcome was going to be. I had also received an email beforehand informing me that the social worker wasn't going to be in the meeting which made me very apprehensive because if anybody was on our side and knew our family well it was her. She knew my mum from before the Alzheimer's got worse and knew what we would do as a family to help her. She had also seen the bond between my parents and this was key to getting her off her section. My dad and I made our way to the hospital for our meeting whilst my friend had Charlotte for me so that I could have my full focus on my mum and her best interests. I will always be thankful for the help with childcare when I needed it so I could focus on my mum and attend meetings without children. My friend never hesitated in offering help and really was a true friend to me whilst times were tough. She helped with school pickups, childcare and advice on many occasions and I will always be truly grateful for that. I don't think people will realise how much some support can really make a huge difference.

As I don't have a huge family and don't have a very big social circle, any support was critical in helping me with the journey I was on.

When we got to the hospital we were sat in a small waiting room, so I nervously just flicked through some dementia magazines. Eventually we were called in. As we walked in I looked around and I felt so nervous and intimidated. There were about 10 people in the room sat around a table. I assumed it was going to be maybe the consultant and one other person, I was not expecting so many people to be there. I felt sick to my stomach because I have always been shy and its only since having my children that I have grown in confidence. With that said I am still very shy and talking in front of 10 people I didn't know was already filling me with dread. If I can avoid large group conversations I will and if I can sit in the background I will do, happily. However, I was here now and to be honest there was nothing going to stop me doing what was needed to help get my mum out of this hospital. I had my dad for support and knew he would do most of the talking so I just tried to ignore the 10 pairs of eyes glaring at me sympathetically.

The meeting was started with everybody introducing themselves one by one. I don't really remember much about who was there but it was the consultant we had to convince. He started off going through what had happened to my mum and the symptoms she expressed. He stated that she had only been sectioned for a short while and that they needed to find a medication to help with the hallucinations and voices. He said that we couldn't have a repeat of what happened when my dad went away and made it very clear that my mum was in the right place and she needed the help they could offer. He asked if my dad wanted to say anything and my dad explained that the decline in mental state was because he went away, and said it probably wouldn't have happened otherwise. He went on to say that he wanted my mum back home because he missed her and she wasn't in the right place. I tilted my head sideways and my eyes filled up. I was conscious of the all the eyes on me but the emotion running through me was taking over any other feelings. It was filling me with grief hearing my dad pour his heart out about feeling lost without her and actually hearing him talking about how he felt. The consultant knew my dad was thinking with his heart and although he looked like he understood why my dad was saying what he was, he was still adamant my mum needed further help and he explained about the section and the laws and rules regarding it. When it seemed like things couldn't get any worse and my hopes had been crushed I decided to do what needed to be done and speak up.

As soon as I started talking that was it, all my emotions came flooding out. Through falling tears and stuttered words I explained how my mum was more lost, more confused and her mental state was declining every single day that she was away from my dad. I explained how she was making no sense when talking to her and that she wasn't getting the love and attention she needed with the disease. I went on to explain that she needed help but that wasn't help that she couldn't have put into place at home. I followed this up with the fact that my dad was going to quit the gym and stay at home with my mum. I also made it very clear that we knew as a family it wouldn't be easy but we wanted to have her being looked after at home for as long as possible because that is where she belonged with her beloved husband. I told the consultant that my dad needed this precious time with my mum and that he was lost without her. We didn't want her spending the next 3 weeks or more in hospital for her to only get worse and then she would end up going from hospital to a home and we were not ready for that yet. I prayed for her to come home through snot and tears. I described how she held onto my dad so tightly when she saw him and the love they still had for one and other was still the same as when they met as teenagers, and that could get them through anything. I was talking from the heart honestly and with passion, and I don't know how but I managed to change the consultants mind. I could see that he truly believed in us taking care of my mum and that was what we wanted. We all knew that some changes would need to be put into place to make her time at home sustainable. He explained that he would put my mum on a holiday from the section which meant she could go home for about 3 days but then we would need to return for another review to see how things were going. If all was well then the section could be lifted, but if it all backfired then she would still have a bed in the hospital as she was still under the section. My dad and I were absolutely ecstatic, the happiness and relief we felt was overwhelming. I couldn't actually believe my mum was going to be allowed home back where she belonged. I was crying my heart out but this time with tears of happiness and all I wanted to do now was give her the good news. However, the consultant went on to explain how some home help would need to be put into place for her so that some of the tension and stress was taken off my dad. He asked what we had in place at home at the moment and my dad explained that nothing was in place. It was decided that we would have a carer come in to look after my mum and this would need to be worked out with the social worker as soon as possible. It was also advised that she was to be given another medication to try. This medication would hopefully help with the psychotic symptoms she was expressing and we were told to start off with half a tablet and then increase it to 1 whole tablet after a few days. It was also explained to us that we would also be given another medication that could be used as and when her behaviour was declining. So if we could see my mum starting to get anxious and looking like she was going to head in the same direction as when she got sectioned then we should give her a tablet. It was a tablet that was supposed to calm her and hopefully help us avoid any more unwanted situations. We were more than happy with that so we agreed and that's when the consultant told us to wait 1 hour so that they could prepare the medication and then we could take my mum back home. We shook the hand of the consultant and thanked everybody in the room before walking out. As we got out of the room and the door shut behind us my dad and I turned to one and other smiling and gave each other a hug of achievement and elation. My dad said to me, 'Nat, that was all your doing, if it wasn't for you saying what you did, he wouldn't have let your mum out. Well done.' I was so happy and proud that I went out of my comfort zone and achieved what I set out to do.

My dad and I went to a nearby coffee shop whilst we waited for the hour to go by so that we could go and collect my mum. I overcame several situations today that I would always avoid in normal circumstances, but for once I was brave and pushed my fears aside and it paid off. I was starting to realise how much more fearless and persistent I was becoming as I was becoming a woman of more responsibilities, one of which being my mum. We got back to the hospital and headed to see her to tell her she would be coming home. She was relieved and you could see the anxiety seep away from her slowly. We left her belongings because we knew we would have to come back in a few days anyway and we walked out of the hospital with a feeling of achievement. That night, myself, my dad, my mum and my two eldest children went to the theatre to see the Wizard of Oz. It was such a happy moment and I was so happy to be sharing moments like that with my mum once again.

The three days went by very quickly, and nothing had really changed. It was like my mum had never been in hospital but also things were still tough just like before she was sectioned. The care wasn't put into place yet as it all had to be done properly and paperwork needed to be completed which was not as straight forward as it sounded. Me and my dad just plodded on caring for my mum and giving her the 24-hour care that she needed. She was not left her own at any point in the day and we both felt really appreciative that she was at home with us even though it was tough. When we went back for the final review, we were pretty confident she would be taken off her section as we hadn't had any further complications and things just seemed to be back to "normal", whatever normal was. This time we were joined by my mum in the review. There wasn't as many professionals in this review and it was quite a short and snappy meeting. I didn't feel as apprehensive about this one because I knew the hardest part had been done and I also had the knowledge that the consultant had stated, if all was well for the 3 days, then she would be taken off her section. Whilst in the review my mum was obviously very anxious again and wasn't too pleased to be back. The consultant asked how things had been and we explained that she had been fine and that the section was just a blip due to my dad's absence. We described how happy she was to be home and we hadn't seen any further decline. He also asked about the care plan and we explained we were still waiting and it was being put into place as soon as it could be.

After several minutes the consultant eventually revealed that my mum's section would be lifted but reassured us that if we needed help not to be afraid to ask. I was so happy and all I kept thinking was, 'I hope I never have to step foot in this hospital ever again.' Eventually the consultant turned to my mum and asked a few questions about how she felt. You could see the confusion in her eyes and she got upset and walked out of the review. Even though she didn't argue or disagree with much, I think deep down she had no understanding of why she had been hospitalised. In her eyes she had done nothing wrong and she had no understanding of the situation. I got up from my chair and followed my mum out of the room and we found a seat outside. Her anxiety had increased so much that she started talking nonsense outside, walking up and down and getting on and off her seat refusing to sit still. She eventually calmed down and sat still but I could see just being in the hospital was making her uneasy and the sooner we could get her home the better.

My dad eventually came out of the meeting and he went to my mum's room to collect all her belongings. When he joined us he informed me that her electric toothbrush was missing. We spoke to a member of staff that told us my mum didn't have an electric toothbrush and it wasn't on the inventory when she was booked in. My dad and I just looked at each other with a, 'can this actually be happening and is this place for real' look because we had both seen the toothbrush in her room previously and I remembered packing it when my mum was sectioned. So the member of staff went to have a look for the toothbrush and eventually found it, which made us question why it wasn't recorded when she was booked in. This also brought to light the rings that went missing as we were previously told only three rings were booked in when she had four. It was quite obvious mistakes were being made and we wanted some answers or an explanation about the whereabouts of the rings and not to just be ignored. Whilst my mum and I waited outside the front of the hospital my dad decided he would speak to a manager. When he eventually came outside about 15 minutes later he explained that the manager had no interest, she just shrugged it off and said he should make an official complaint. This was the second time the staff were unempathetic and not very helpful when questioned on the whereabouts of my mum's property. It was decided a short while after that we would file a police report just so that the hospital could see that we were not going to just be fobbed off and we would do something about it. We were fully aware that nothing would be able to be done because there was no evidence and the chances were the rings were long gone but we just wanted to pursue it because of the manager and the staff's lack of understanding and care. The main priority right now was getting my mum back home and away from this hospital. I was so happy to see her getting in the car and driving away from there for the last time and not stuck behind the same walls without anything to keep her mind occupied. However, it wasn't much longer before her freedom was to be taken from her once again and she was to be stuck behind four walls once again.

Medication Is Given to Help, Right?

Once back at home and settled in days went by one by one, each day similar to the one before. The home help still hadn't been put into place, and me and my dad were still coping with just the two of us most of the time. My dad was doing his exercise at home which meant I was no longer needed to go and sit round whilst he went to the gym but that didn't stop me going round every evening to change bedding, wash my mum, take dinner, or just to go and see everything was OK. I was still taking my mum out in the day and sometimes in the evening. Whether it was to a shop, for lunch or dinner, just to keep her occupied and to stop her mind going into overdrive. She had started her new medication but we were not noticing any changes yet. My dad coped so well with spending most of all day every day with my mum. Most days involved cleaning up faeces off her body or cleaning up the mess in the bathroom after she had attempted to clean herself up. After a few weeks of feeling like she had reached some sort of plateau with the disease, we noticed she started becoming quite sluggish. She was spending a lot of time on the sofa resting and the majority of the time it was with her eyes closed. Trying to walk the dogs with her was becoming a huge strain on me and it was no longer enjoyable. She was walking slower than my feet would allow and my patience would accept. I was finding myself becoming short with her and urging her to be quicker. To me it was like she couldn't be bothered but what I didn't realise was that there was more to it than that. If I would have known she wasn't just being lazy then maybe I would have been more patient, however maybe I should have realised by now that nothing was ever straight forward with Alzheimer's.

As days went by my mum became more and more sleepy and increasingly sluggish with her movements. It seemed to me like she was less with it and was less able to hold a conversation. She was now unable to make her own drink, she would open the fridge and forget what she had opened it for, my dad would walk into the kitchen and all the cupboard doors were open. I even once saw her so desperate for a drink that she was trying to drink a beer out of the fridge with the cap on. She couldn't work out why she wasn't getting any drink from the bottle and got a bit tearful but I soon helped her by making her a glass of juice and giving it to her. My mum has never liked beer so I believe she just grabbed the first liquid drink she could find. It was getting increasingly difficult for my dad and I at this point because everything seemed twice as hard to manage. Trying to get her in the shower was bad enough to start with but now with her lethargic movements and lack of co-ordination it was near on impossible. Trying to lift a heavy fully grown woman into a shower over a bath tub would be difficult but trying to co-ordinate them, hold them up and wash them at the same time was beyond problematic. My mum had a couple of small falls in the shower, bumped her head and also turned the dial to control the temperature herself and ended up with a small scold patch above her eye where she turned the water too hot.

With my mum becoming lethargic and less aware we started thinking about how we could make all our lives a little bit easier. We needed a walk-in shower for my mum to make the care more manageable and her routine more comfortable. We looked into it and after numerous meetings with different people we were told that my dad would have to fund the shower himself as he owned a house and had money going into the bank each month. My dad does have a decent income but looking into the cost of a shower being built suitable for somebody with a disability wasn't something my dad could just scrabble together and get done anytime soon and we needed it now. The social worker tried to help but there was nothing she could do. My dad was so hurt at the lack of help for my mum so me and Shaun decided he would put the shower in for my dad. Shaun is not a plumber or a bathroom installer, he's an electrician, but he is good at most jobs around the house. He may not fit a shower to a professional standard but he could do the job and it would work out a fraction of the price just getting the materials. So we let my dad know that if he got the materials needed for the walk-in shower, Shaun would fit it for him as soon as he next could. We waited until the end of the month to order the materials and then planned for Shaun to do the work when my dad had some time away in a couple of weeks. Shaun booked the annual leave from work so that he had the time to complete such a large task. That was a relief for my dad and I because it would be one less thing we would have to struggle with daily.

The social worker was aware of my mum's sluggish behaviour and we were told to just keep an eye on her. Being sleepier was another symptom of Alzheimer's but it just felt too soon for her to be this tired all the time. We started thinking, was the new medication making her decline? Surely another medication wasn't having a negative impact on her again, she can't be that unlucky!

Then one evening my mum was in bed and my dad heard a huge thud. He ran upstairs and she had fell out of bed and by the looks of it she had hit her head. She was rubbing the back of her head, and said she banged it when asked. My dad made sure she was OK and she didn't seem to upset by the fall. She went to bed that evening and it was just like any normal night. When my mum woke up the following morning she seemed just like she had been over the last few weeks. She was slow, un-coordinated, and sleepy. I rang my dad that morning and he suggested going into town as he needed to go into the bank, so I agreed. We parked the car up on the outskirts of town and started the 5-minute walk into the town centre. I remember this day so clearly because I had seen my mum walking slow when we walked the dogs but she had taken the slow walking to another level. She was so slow and unsteady that the 5-minute walk took about 20 minutes. She was so lethargic and her speech was sounding very slow and slightly slurred too. Me and my dad both expressed our concerns to each other but it was so hard to know when something was wrong when we didn't know what to expect with the illness. Was it normal or was something happening that we should be concerned about? This was such unfamiliar territory to us and it felt like we had experienced such a bad decline with my mum that we would normally just accept the bad because it was part and parcel of what we were dealing with. On this occasion something in my gut was telling me something wasn't quite right.

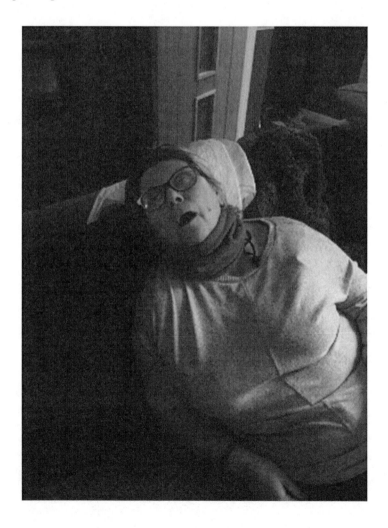

We eventually got to the bank and we had a 10-minute wait for a member of staff. We sat down to wait and after a few minutes my mum had fell asleep in the chair. After the bank we then went to Costa for breakfast and whilst I was waiting to be served she sat in a chair and fell asleep again. Something felt really wrong, she was never this tired and it wasn't often she fell asleep in a public place. Once we got her hot chocolate and porridge we started to realise the full extent of how bad she really was. My mum had always been able to put spoon to mouth and pick up her drinks. She sometimes made a mess but she was always able, however on this occasion she wasn't. Not only could she not do the simplest things but she was so much more confused than normal and not able to process anything. She was trying to drink the porridge and couldn't pick up her spoon. She then did something that crushed my heart once again. I was so shocked and felt like I was watching the Alzheimer's taking my mum away piece by piece in front of me. She was using an imaginary spoon and either placing it in her porridge or her hot chocolate and then slowly raising it to her mouth. She slowly took a mouthful of nothing, like a tortoise takes a bite of its food. She was eating nothing and then repeating the action. My dad at this point was helping her by spoon feeding her whilst she continued to raise her hand to her mouth with nothing in it. Something I wasn't ready to see yet, my mum being spoon fed. At one point to make light of the situation my dad asked her, 'is that nice, is that better than the porridge I'm feeding you.' We all let out a little much needed laugh, even though I had all sorts of thoughts flying around in my head. Was this it? Was my mum unable to feed herself or stay awake? Could life be that cruel? Even the way she was walking around was unsettling, she had her mouth half open like she couldn't shut it but wasn't opening it fully. So after an upsetting morning my dad took her back home.

A few hours later I got a call off my dad who was beside himself. He explained to me that something wasn't right and he didn't know what to do. He said my mum had slept most of the time she was at home and he said she didn't look well. So I jumped in my car and went round to my parent's house. When I got there I was shocked and disturbed by what I saw. She was slumped on the sofa with her mouth wide open, she looked run down and any colour she did have was drained from her skin. Upon closer observation I noticed my mum's mouth was drooped on one side, and when she eventually woke up she was slurring her words so badly that we started becoming concerned about the fall out of bed she had the previous night. My dad was adamant something wasn't right so we decided that I should try and get some advice from somewhere. I tried ringing the social worker but she didn't answer so I emailed her explaining what had happened that day and I phoned the doctors who said they would ring back. The doctors are not always great at phoning back when they say they will so this wasn't a call I was going to wait for without trying to get help from elsewhere. I then rang the dementia crisis helpline and they explained to me that their system was down and they would phone me back, but they never did. I was getting a bit restless because I didn't know where I could turn and I needed to know from a professional that my mum was going to be OK. Eventually a social worker phoned me and put their manager on. After I explained about the fall out of bed she advised I got medical help. I rang 111 and from the information I gave them they decided it was best they send an ambulance out to come and check my mum over. I felt a sense of relief because I knew she would have all the appropriate observations done and then we could relax.

After a short period of time the ambulance arrived and I let the two crew members in. They asked questions about the Alzheimer's and how advanced my mum's was. We informed them of all the symptoms she was expressing that she normally didn't. They also asked my mum a few questions, one of which was who I was. She looked quite confused and said I was her mum. This was very unusual because she knew who I was and had never once called me her mum before. They did some of the routine checks like blood pressure and heart rate and then they assessed her physically. They asked her to push with both of her arms, and concluded that one arm was slightly weaker, the same side that was drooping on her mouth. Once they completed the assessment they decided it was best she went into hospital. They explained that with the drooping of the mouth, the weakness on one side and the knock to the head, it could have been a possibility that mum had suffered a stroke. They couldn't say with one hundred percent certainty what was wrong with her but they said she definitely needed checking over at the hospital. My mum's anxiety increased as soon as the ambulance showed up, so I knew she would be stressed about getting onto it. I didn't want her to worry because this wasn't like last time but her last experience made her wary and nervous of seeing healthcare professionals. I explained to her that she needed to go to hospital and that I would go with her, luckily Shaun was at home for the children. My dad chose not to go with us because he was very upset at the whole situation. His PTSD peaks when he's stressed and I knew he wouldn't deal very well with waiting around and receiving any unwelcome news, if that was to happen. I knew I would deal with the situation better than my dad and I was fully aware on a Friday night I would be in for a long night. My mum willingly got helped onto a chair so that she could be transported to the ambulance and we both got belted into the back. I told my dad I would keep him updated.

When we got to the hospital I could see it was very busy, the corridors had people lined up in beds waiting to go to where they needed to be. My mum was added to the queue and it was a long painful wait. An hour of waiting in the corridor we were taken to the emergency assessment unit, where she had her bloods taken and an ECG. She was getting quite tearful at this point but I tried to reassure her everything would be OK. We then got moved to a cubicle where a doctor came round and she explained that she wanted my mum to have a CT scan because of the knock to the head. Whilst she was there she also informed me that she didn't think my mum had suffered a stroke. I believe the bloods and ECG were all fine and the doctor said that the symptoms were not obvious enough to be a stroke. This was a relief to me because having a stroke on top of dealing with the Alzheimer's wasn't really ideal, however I was still looking for answers regarding my mum's rapid decline. Whilst she was sat waiting to go for her CT scan she did appear to be improving slightly, she wasn't slurring as much and her mouth had straightened out. She was making conversation even if most of what she said didn't make much sense, that wasn't abnormal though. Eventually my mum was taken down for a CT scan, and I was feeling slightly apprehensive about getting her into the machine. I knew it wouldn't be easy because not only was her co-ordination poor but she also hated small spaces and feeling like she was closed in somewhere so I knew it would be a challenge. When we got into the room I helped her off the bed and tried to get her to sit on the part of the machine where she would eventually be laying down. She sat on the edge, but every time I tried to get her to swivel round and lay on her back she panicked and refused. I tried several times and tried to reassure her that it would be done quickly and she would be fine but she started shaking and getting upset. After several attempts at persuading her the lady that was going to do the scan said it was best we left it because she wasn't going to lay down and be still. So I got her back on her bed and she was taken back to the cubicle she was in. It was now nearly p.m. and after several hours at the hospital I was told my mum would be kept in overnight. I took her to the toilet, and put her back into the bed and she fell asleep. That was my opportunity to get home and get some sleep as I was exhausted and drained, so I rang my dad and he collected me from the hospital and dropped me home.

Out of The Frying Pan And Into The Fire

The next morning I woke up and I knew I needed to go and visit my mum and find out how she was after a night in the hospital. My dad and I went straight to the hospital after grabbing some breakfast and were quite taken aback by what we saw when we arrived. She had her own space on a ward and she was just sat in the chair that was beside her bed. Considering on the Friday evening she appeared to be improving slightly, it was like she had taken another 5 steps back. Her words were slurred again, she was very confused and the guilt I was riddled with for leaving my mum that night was huge. She had obviously deteriorated over night and I was now starting to worry. What was happening? What was going to happen next? I had Charlotte with me and my mum didn't really acknowledge that, she seemed to be on a completely different planet and not aware of her surroundings at all. My dad sat her upright, gave her a drink and just held her hand. I asked the doctor what was happening and they spoke about the new medication that she was on, stating that it could have been causing the adverse effects. However, they also still wanted to get a CT scan done because this would rule out anything we couldn't see after she had the hit to the head. My dad went down with my mum to get the CT scan done and he managed to keep her happy and calm enough to get it done this time, another example of the strength of their connection. We would need to wait for the results and the doctor explained she would be staying for the foreseeable until she improved or they could find the exact cause of the decline. Whilst we were there the lady with the hospital food came around with her trolley. She asked my mum what she wanted to eat and she just stared and muttered some unrelated words to the lady. She wasn't even able to choose her food for lunch, which massively concerned me because when she didn't have me or my dad by her side who would be able to make these choices for her? Who was going to make sure she was cared for and was getting enough food and fluid? She was in a hospital on the emergency assessment unit not in a dementia hospital or in a place where they had the knowledge about dementia to help. I was so relieved I was by her side on this occasion because it meant I was there to order for her. I had spent so much time with her I knew what she liked and didn't like and what food would be easier for her to eat. The food was placed in front of her and she was unable to pick up her fork, so I fed her. I told the nurses I was concerned that if I wasn't there, she wouldn't eat as she was unable to feed herself. They said they would make sure she was eating and drinking and for me not to worry. I know I should be more willing to accept peoples promises and words but I had no faith that my mum would be looked after the way I felt she should. She only had a few mouthfuls of her lunch and then said she was done. I was also informed she had only had a few mouthfuls of cornflakes in the morning for breakfast too. This was always a great fear of mine with my mum, not eating enough food, her energy levels dropping and then getting weaker. Our bodies need food to function and when your body isn't functioning well anyway, the last thing it needs is to be deprived of food too. I could see she was too weak and confused to eat and that was worrying me greatly. We sat and spoke to my mum for quite a while and she was not only incoherent most of the time but when she did manage to get a full sentence out it made no sense what so ever. She was speaking about her house key and how she was going to meet me downstairs, and obviously I just nodded my head because I didn't really know how to react or what to say. I informed her that she would need to stay in the hospital until the doctor had checked her over, and she was so unaware that she just accepted what was happening without any worries. My dad gave her a kiss and we walked away.

The following day I was hoping to see some improvement so that my mum could come home but that wasn't to be the case. She appeared to look the same as the day before. As soon as I got to her she told me she needed a toilet, so I got her up from the chair and took the very slow walk to the toilet just up the corridor. When we got into the toilet I told her to take her knickers down and to sit on the toilet. She looked so confused and was very unsteady on her feet. I had charlotte with me and was trying to hold charlotte and make sure my mum didn't lose her balance. I eventually managed to use one hand to take her knickers down and I could see her incontinence pad was full of urine, so full that it needed changing. I was then trying to get her to sit on the toilet but she couldn't follow the instructions I was giving. She kept slightly bending like she was about to sit on the floor and then would go to pull her knickers up. After numerous times of asking my mum to sit on the toilet and not getting anywhere near it, I started to get frustrated and upset. I was confused how a few days ago she was getting on the toilet herself when she wanted and now she wasn't even able to sit on it. I started to feel useless because I couldn't help my mum and I didn't know what to do. Using one hand to try and get somebody on the toilet that has no co-ordination and the inability to follow instructions was impossible. I placed my mum's hand on a rail in the toilet and told her to hold on, as I peeped my head out of the door. Luckily a nurse was passing by and I asked her if she could help me. Once the nurse came into the toilet I was so frustrated, angry and upset that I said I was leaving and walked out. As soon as the toilet door closed behind me I walked off crying my eyes out. I couldn't quite believe what was happening, I was annoyed at myself for getting frustrated and my concern was growing each day for my mum. Was this just another decline? A sharp drop down the dark hole that is Alzheimer's. I was scared.

As if I thought things couldn't get any worse, the next day would be a day I would never ever forget. I have had some days with my mum that have upset me, made me worry and stressed but this was the first day I thought I was losing her right in front of me, it was the end of the fight. It was by far the most upsetting scene I've witnessed in my life and won't be one I will forget anytime soon. I received a phone call that morning and was informed my mum had fell out of her chair and she had banged her top lip, which didn't make me feel assured that she was in a safe place. This made me apprehensive about my visit and worried about what I was going to see when I got there. The social worker had contacted me and was going to meet my dad and I at the hospital because she wanted to see how things were going. As I walked onto the ward I could see my mum laying upright on the bed, asleep with her eyes rolling in her head. Her mouth was wide open and she kept waking up for a few seconds muttering and then half nodding off again. She looked grey, her lips were chapped and a shade of grey/blue. As I walked closer to her I could see the massive bloodied lump on her lip which straight away stirred my emotions. I felt like I was looking at a corpse. Why was my un-coordinated mum allowed to sit in a chair with nothing holding her in when she was sleepy? The floors were solid and I could only imagine how scared and confused she was when she saw the floor coming towards her face. All that kept going through my head was, is this how it ends? Is this my lasting image of my mum? Is this her now? I'm going to be visiting her in a home and watching her sleep and mutter and never be able to have a conversation with her again. Does she even know who I am? The social worker gave me a concerned look and asked how I was. I told her that I was confused with what was happening and asked if the Alzheimer's could really go downhill as quickly as it appeared to be with my mum. She said that her decline was very unusual but at the same time everyone is different and Alzheimer's is different with every case. She was concerned about her obvious lack of fluids, her lips looked like they hadn't touched water for hours and hours. I sat down on the chair next to my mum's bed and waited for my dad who was parking the car, and he also had Charlotte. I didn't want to be upset when he got there so I tried to fight back the tears and upset. Today was a day that I was not strong enough to hold back those tears. The image of my mum disturbed me so much and the reality of what we were facing really hit me hard. I knew my dad would struggle seeing her in such a bad state that I wanted to be strong for him. I heard my dad walking down the corridor with Charlotte in the wrong direction of the ward, so I shouted to divert him. He came back and proceeded to head towards us.

As soon as he saw her I knew from his expression he was upset, as much as he thinks it's well-hidden, I've seen it far too often recently to not recognise it. He always wears his dark shades so his eyes cannot be seen, but I can see the frown lines above his eyes, the expression of a broken man. That in turn upset me because I knew there was nothing I could do to change what was happening. He stayed a few minutes and sat beside my mum on her bed. The nurse came passed and the social worker expressed her concerns, she explained that my mum wasn't able to fill a cup from a jug herself and that she wouldn't drink herself without help. The nurse explained that my mum should have had a red lid on her jug so that everybody was aware she needed assistance. This was so frustrating to hear because it was pretty obvious she wasn't able to do things for herself and I felt like she was just another patient in a bed and she wasn't receiving the detailed and close up care she needed. The nurse also explained that my mum hadn't woke up for breakfast and wasn't eating or drinking because she was asleep most of the time. The social worker said that she should have been woken for meals and drinks because it wasn't good for her to be going without essentials. My dad and I tried to wake her whilst the nurse went to go and get some porridge and a hot chocolate for her. My mum was so unresponsive apart from the odd eyelid opening slightly and a slight mutter every now and again. She just kept closing her eyes and laying down. After about 10 minutes we decided we needed to physically pick her up to sit her up and then maybe she would open her eyes for a little longer. We eventually managed to wake her and I cannot express how I felt at that time. She could barely move her lips, her eyes were only just about open, and she looked severely unwell. She couldn't talk, she couldn't stand up unaided, she couldn't pick a spoon or a cup up. My beloved mother appeared to be completely brain dead, I was crushed. We all sat there in silence until my dad stood up and walked out saying he couldn't do it. I knew my dad wouldn't be able to cope with what was happening, and I was just about keeping it together. I honestly felt like my mum was disappearing in front of me and I didn't understand why. I sat on the chair next to her and held Charlotte close to me. I hid my head behind hers and finally released all the emotion I was fighting to hold in. I kept wiping away the tears one by one hoping nobody would notice that I was crying. My heart was shattered and the only thing keeping me from breaking down hysterically was my beautiful girl in my arms and watching her smiling away at everybody. The lady came back with the food for my mum and I fed her and made sure she had a drink, whilst contemplating what was in store for us over the next few days. The social worker expressed her concern to a doctor about my mum and he advised that her new medication that she started was to be stopped. He did express that she was showing classic symptoms of Alzheimer's but we tried to make him understand that this wasn't normal for my mum. I understood things could go downhill but I could never have imagined it would be this quickly.

After feeling utterly heartbroken and distraught I was really anxious about going to the hospital the next day. If my mum had declined further, I don't think I could have actually coped. I honestly started to feel like I was going to see her on her death bed and was praying for a miracle of some sort. When I got to the hospital the following day she still wasn't great but she had improved slightly, I was so relieved I felt a glimmer of hope that her current state wasn't permanent. She was still very uncoordinated and her actions and words were still very muddled. Whilst I was there that day I fed my mum her dinner as she still wasn't able to use the cutlery to feed herself. She definitely had more life in her though, she was talking less slurred and she had a bit of colour back in her cheeks. However, one of my main concerns was my mum's care and the understanding of the care she needed considering she had Alzheimer's. The jug she had on her side still had the wrong-coloured lid on it and her lips were still very dry and she was clearly dehydrated still. Although the staff were lovely and worked amazingly hard, I did feel my mum's basic needs were not being met. When the dinner trolley came round and I wasn't present, I am assuming they asked her what she wanted and if she didn't answer or make any sense then they just guessed. When I got to the hospital there was a meal I knew my mum wouldn't eat sat cold on the side. Somebody would then come round and take the meal away probably assuming she wasn't hungry. Luckily I was there for most of the meal times because I could ask for the meal I knew my mum would eat and also assist her with it. It concerned me that whilst I wasn't there she was probably just being left to her own devices and treated like every other patient. The lack of understanding frustrates me quite often, and I never felt happy about anybody else caring for my mum. Whenever she was away from home in somebody else's care, she never received the care she would have been getting at home. I know my mum so well and have learned to anticipate tears before they fall, anxiety before she breaks, and an illness before its diagnosed. That's because spending almost every day with her since she became ill, I have learnt to understand my mum and what she needs and wants. I have learned so much more about Alzheimer's seeing it first-hand and it's not just as simple as losing your memory or forgetting things like many have assumed.

My dad came up to the hospital to see my mum and he was so overjoyed that my she seemed to have improved slightly. Whilst we were both there we were told that she wouldn't be able to come home until measures were put into place. She needed to be safe and secure and they said a review would take place the following day to see if my mum had improved anymore. The occupational therapist came and spoke to us about how they could help and what could be put into place. It was decided that an alarm system would be put on the front door so that my dad would hear if my mum tried walking out of the house on her own. My dad was also going to be given a commode chair to keep downstairs if my mum was unable to go up the stairs to the toilet, a frame to be placed around the toilet upstairs so she had support if needed and a bed rail and wet sensor mat to be placed on the bed. We were grateful that these things were going to be put into place but annoyed that it seemed to have taken my mum to become ill or put into hospital before anything was done. We explained that we were still waiting for carers to be put into place and we didn't know when this would be done. My dad was keen for my mum to come home well, and also for all the help to be put into place as soon as it could because he only had about a week until he was going away for 2 weeks on a trip to the Falkland's that had been planned for a few years. We had planned it so that my aunty Sue would come down from Manchester and stay at my parent's house with my mum, so my dad wanted it to be made as easy as it could be for her before he went away.

A few days after being admitted my sister went to see my mum and I told her to find out about the CT scan my mum had done. She rang me later on and informed me that the scan had come back all clear which I thought would be the case because we hadn't heard otherwise. The following day my dad and I went back to the hospital with high hopes that my mum would be able to go home. When we saw her we both couldn't believe our eyes, my mum was sat up, talking and not muttering or slurring, and was able to stand up steady on her feet. She was smiling and happy again, which was amazing to see after what we had witnessed the last few days. It was as if the events previously hadn't even happened, she was back to what was considered normal for her with the Alzheimer's. I was elated because it meant things were definitely looking good for her coming home, and all the worries and concerns I had, were lowering to a more manageable level. The occupational therapist came over to talk to us and said she needed to take my mum away just to check how steady she was on her feet. She was going to see if she was capable of climbing upstairs without too much assistance and to check it wasn't too much of a hazard.

When they got back the occupational therapist informed us that my mum passed with flying colours, however she also said that she should be assisted and that we needed to follow her up and down the stairs so that she had some extra support. We were more than happy to listen to any advice given and were just happy that my she was able to come home. A few hours later the doctor came round to just clarify what was happening. He explained that the medication my mum was on was probably the cause for her hospital stay. He explained that it was slowly coming out of her system and hence the reason for her improvement. Although we both hoped that the medication was going to be the cause, we couldn't actually believe how much of an adverse effect it had on her, it was scary. We were just relieved that it wasn't a permanent state for her and so glad she was smiling again. We all said our goodbyes, thanked all the staff and we left the hospital just in time for me to pick the kids up from school.

Whilst The Cats Away The Mice Will Play

It wasn't long after the hospital stay that the day of my dad's Falkland's trip approached. Originally my mum was going to go to Manchester for the 2 weeks and would be looked after by family but her family said they couldn't cope and it was decided it was best to keep her in her own environment that she was familiar with at home. My aunty Sue said she would come to Colchester and stay at my parent's house to look after my mum. Shaun had a week booked off to install the walk-in shower which also enabled me to be able to sleep at my parents' house to support both my mum and my aunty because the kids had him at home in the morning. Shaun picked my aunty up from Manchester and my dad said his goodbyes, I told him to enjoy himself and appreciate the break. He knew my mum was in good hands with my aunty and I. My aunty had a list of things she wanted to do for my dad whilst he was gone including cleaning his house from top to bottom and chasing the social worker about the carers that should have been put into place by now. The door alarm, bed rail and wet mat were still not installed either which wasn't great considering we were told time and time again the house had to be safe for my mum when she was in the hospital. We had the commode and the toilet frame both of which me and my sister picked up the day after she was let out of hospital. We never used the commode as it was never needed because she was always able to walk the stairs with assistance, but the toilet frame was helpful for my mum's co-ordination when trying to get onto the toilet.

We tried to keep my mum's days to a routine and fulfilled so that she didn't have enough time for her mind to go into overdrive. We went to Costa most mornings and had our breakfast like she would have with my dad if he was there. Shaun was cracking on with the walk-in shower so we tried to leave him to it and stay out of his way as much as we could whilst the noisy work was taking place. It didn't take him long to rip the old bath out and start putting the walk-in shower in place. It was so nice having my aunty down, she was like a breath of fresh air. She is very good with my mum anyway but she also wasn't at the end of her tether like my dad and I were sometimes because we had to cope day in day out. It made me feel quite relieved I had her there and also more relaxed because I knew my mum would be more willing to listen to instructions given by my aunty. It sometimes felt like she didn't like being told what to do by her daughter because she was my mother and it should have been the other way round. What she didn't realise was that I was just trying to protect her. When the evening times came round I slept in the spare room and my mum and aunty slept in the double bed together. This was to prevent my mum from rolling out of the bed or trying to walk downstairs in the dark in the middle of the night.

It sounds really odd but it was like a girly holiday, we laughed, we spoke about their pasts, and we ate chocolate EVERY night. Although, we had my mum to take care of, I felt less pressure not having to take her out on my own and it was a nice break from not splitting myself between two households. I picked the kids up from school which is round the corner from my parents but the majority of my time was spent at my parent's house. Shaun fed, bathed, and sorted the kids ready for bed every night whilst I wasn't there. My aunty and I took my mum to the beach for a walk, we went out for lunch several times, we went to the local jam factory where my mum polished off two scones with jam and cream and we went out for walks with the dogs to keep us busy. It was the most I had smiled and laughed with my mum for a while and that was all down to my aunty. She was so chilled and we dealt with any difficulties together. Not only that but she was excellent with the kids, she helped by looking after them whilst I popped home and got my washing on or gave the house a quick clean. She made sure Shaun was fed and watered whilst he was installing the shower and also cooked the most delicious pasta dinner for my mum and I.

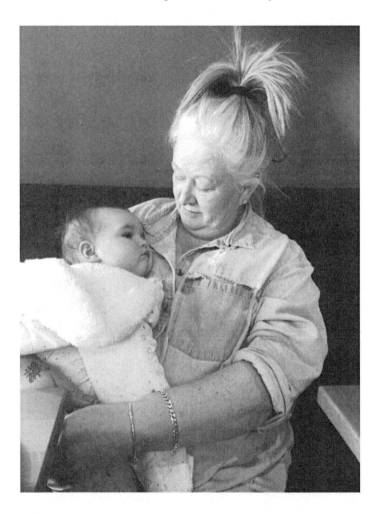

My mum was manageable whilst my dad was away, it was nothing like previous times he wasn't around. She had the odd occasion when she wanted to walk out of places and my aunty and I managed to keep her calm and ensure her everything was OK. All in all it was good though, she seemed calm in her own home and wasn't on edge like she was sometimes when I was on my own with her and my dad was absent. I think the busy days tired her out so she didn't have the energy to start walking off once home and I think she respected my aunty enough to listen and stay within the house when asked to. My mum and aunty have known each other for many years, they were friends before my parents became an item. They went to school together, worked together and caused trouble together. I think this also helped with keeping my mum more relaxed because they had so much to talk and think about, as it wasn't often we got to see my aunty.

As a few days passed it was becoming apparent that my mum was becoming more agitated in the evening times. It started off with her asking if we were there yet even though we weren't going anywhere and asking if we were getting off. She was talking about a train and was worried because she didn't know if she needed to get off. My aunty and I were so confused because she was OK for the most part of the day and then she was talking absolute nonsense that didn't make any sense. I was thinking surely she can see we are not on a train and we are sat in the living room? After a few evenings I started to see that it was around the same time every evening that she started to become more unstable and on edge. Initially we would just say to my mum that we were fine and if she asked if we were staying on we would just answer yes. This seemed to work for the first few nights and with some reassurance the unusual behaviour would just bypass.

Half way through the 2 weeks my dad was away, the social worker had arranged a visit to come and see us all and to see how things were going. When she arrived she could see that my mum was a lot calmer than when my dad last went away and she seemed to be doing OK. My aunty and I explained to the social worker how she appeared to get slightly more anxious and unpredictable in the evenings around the p.m. time. We were very surprised to hear that it was quite normal for people with dementia to experience something called "sundowning". She told us in plain words that sundowning was also known as "late day confusion" and that it was when agitation and confusion got worse in the late afternoon and evening. It could possibly be caused by the disturbance to the 24-hour body clock which is triggered by the physical changes to the brain.

Symptoms could include fear, disorientation, pacing and wandering, anxiety and agitation, and visual and auditory hallucinations. This made so much sense now because the behaviour my mum was presenting was so much more heightened and bizarre than in the day. We were relieved that there was an explanation and just awaited what was to come that following evening now we knew to expect something out of the ordinary.

Whilst the social worker was visiting, my aunty also asked about the carers and said these needed to be put into place before my dad came home because he needed the extra help. It was explained that it was being put into place but she was just waiting for some paperwork to come back before it could start. My aunty explained that my dad would need a carer each morning so that my mum could be washed and changed ready for her day. This also meant that if she soiled in the night my dad wouldn't need to deal with that himself first thing in the morning. She also stated that my dad wanted a cleaner in the house maybe a few times a week so that he could concentrate on my mum and the house was kept clean. At the time, I was going round when I could to clean and change beddings but I didn't do it often enough. I found it so hard trying to fit everything in and cleaning my own house was bad enough without trying to clean somebody else's. I felt like I didn't have the time or the energy. There were occasions where I was cleaning my dad's on a Sunday evening rather than chilling with my family and my house needed a good clean too. The social worker explained that hopefully that could all be put into place but it would just depend on what availability the agency had. She said she would be in touch and hopefully it would be put into place before my dad came home.

A few evenings later my mum's behaviour in the evenings was getting increasingly worse. One night was particularly bad that I remember it like it was yesterday. She started off talking about being on a train again and me and my aunty just tried to keep our answers short and sweet so that we didn't confuse her but also so that we weren't encouraging what was happening. She kept asking if we were getting off the train and then started getting upset because she didn't know if she needed to get off the train. My aunty eventually decided to tell my mum that she was home and everything was OK, but she obviously wasn't seeing what we were. We tried to get my mum to look around and showed her some pictures on the wall and explained that she was at home. She got more and more upset and once she had started there was no going back. She became really anxious and starting panicking, pulling at her top and saying she couldn't breathe. We tried our best to calm her and told her she was OK but she was starting to have a panic attack. We took her top off and her bra as she was feeling restricted by wearing anything and we opened the windows in the living room. It was cold but we wanted her to feel the fresh air so that she didn't feel so confined. My mum kept looking like she was going to calm down and then she started crying again and got worked up once more. I walked into the kitchen to get a drink and that's when I saw her medication on the side. It reminded me that my mum had the medication she was prescribed when she first got sectioned. We were told to use it as and when we felt she needed calming down, and this was one of those times. I cleared it with my aunty before making the decision to give my mum half of one of those tablets in the hope it would help her become more relaxed. She continued getting upset and needed consoling for about 20 minutes and then she eventually calmed down. It was definitely the worst night of the 2 weeks and at the time we were really scared for her. Whatever was going through her head at that moment in time was obviously very disturbing and upsetting and it made me feel quite useless because I couldn't help when I didn't know what was a reality for my mum. My aunty was very good, she didn't panic, didn't get frustrated, and just did her best to talk to her and divert her mind elsewhere. Something that proved much more difficult on this occasion.

Apart from the odd night that was a little more difficult than others, my mum coped very well without my dad being at home. However, I definitely felt that my knowledge of her illness helped in situations that my aunty would have otherwise struggled. I think we both used each other to lean on and we both gave each other the support and backup required when facing an unknown situation. We never knew what was going to happen next with my mum or whether the next day would be worse than the day before. When Shaun was due back to work after his 9 days off my aunty expressed her concern that I would not be sleeping at my parent's house. As he left for work at 6a.m. I needed to sleep at home so that I would be home for the kids and then I would need to get the kids sorted before I could go round to help. I understood how my aunty felt because when you have support it gives you so much more strength and confidence to take on whatever a day throws at you. I rang Shaun and explained how my aunty felt and he said he would see what he could do. A few hours later he phoned me and told me that his boss understood the situation and had allowed him to take another week's holiday so that I could sleep at my parent's house for the remainder of the time until my dad was home. My aunty was so happy when she found out and said she felt more relaxed knowing I would be with her to help. It also gave Shaun another week to complete the walk-in shower and get it looking good.

The days went by quickly and the day my dad was coming home soon arrived. We explained to my mum that my dad was coming home and she was pleased. She wasn't as happy as she would have been in the past if she hadn't seen him for 2 weeks but she was happy. My mum had asked about him a few times whilst he was gone and when we explained he had gone to the Falkland's she was OK with that. We were also sure to tell her that the reason he had gone on his own without her was because he had to go on a plane and she didn't like flying. She didn't seem to express any upset that he wasn't there but at the same time it was obvious she was thinking about him because she kept asking where he was. When my dad walked through the door he gave my mum a big hug and she gave him a half-hearted hug back. I thanked my aunty for all her help and support by treating her to a hot water dispenser (my dad has one and she loved it) and said my goodbyes. I was going to miss our girly nights and the laughs we had together. These days and evenings together were so precious and the smiles we saw from my mum's face were priceless.

The next day everything was back to how it should be. My dad was refreshed after his 2-week break, my aunty was back in Manchester and my mum had a brand-new walk-in shower to make things that little bit easier. She was settled back into her routine with my dad, but it was only a few weeks before the dreaded decline hit us again and we were struggling to cope once more.

The Care Amended, the Disease Degraded

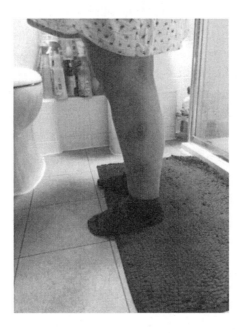

After a few weeks of my dad being settled back into his caring role for my mum, he received a call to arrange the installation of the door alarm, the bed rail and the wet mat for the mattress. They also said they would put a grab rail in the shower. These were all installed within a few days of the call and helped put my dad's mind at ease slightly. We knew my mum would be safe in bed and wouldn't have another fall like last time. However, the bed wasn't the only place she could fall over and hurt herself. She started falling quite easily in the street and it was proving much more difficult for her to coordinate just 1 or 2 steps. We had to make sure we had hold of her for support if we went out but it wasn't always easy to prevent a fall because she isn't the lightest of ladies. My mum had a couple of small falls down the stairs at home. She would miss a step or two on the way down but luckily enough she was always nearer the bottom than the top, so never hurt herself too much as far as I was aware. I say as far as I was aware because since her hospital visits, all the doctors' appointments and social worker visits she became more secretive about any pain or illnesses she had. I believe she associated any hurt or sickness with going away and she didn't want to have to go away again. Her experiences were not great and I didn't blame her for worrying. She would always say she was OK even when she obviously wasn't, but it was just a case of thoroughly checking her over if she did have a fall and watching her posture, facial expressions and actions closely.

One day my dad and I took my mum out for the morning. We went to a shop to have a look around and we decided to go upstairs, so we headed towards the escalator. My parents were ahead whilst I was browsing the shelves, and they held hands as they stepped onto the escalator together. The next thing I knew I saw my mum crashing down the escalator step by step from about half way up. I was frantic and didn't know what to do apart from shouting the word mum over and over. I froze in horror at what I was seeing, I was trembling and was so scared for her. My dad was shouting to hit the button and after a few drawn out and traumatic seconds, another customer hit the emergency stop button. I ran over to my mum and got help to lift her up. I was filled with dread straight away because I just kept thinking she cannot have come out of that unscathed. My eyes filled with tears and I couldn't get that image of her rolling down sharp metal steps out of my head. I just remembered thinking she was already too fragile for something like this to happen to her, I was angry that it did. It didn't take long for staff to come running over as they heard the commotion and they said they would get a first aider to have a look at my mum. At a first glance she appeared absolutely fine physically, she was a bit unsettled and confused but she seemed fine otherwise. The staff got a stool for her to sit on whilst my dad and I just stood next to her still is absolute shock that this had happened. My mum was stating that she was OK and I explained the situation including the fact that she wasn't great at expressing her feelings or if she was hurt. They tried moving her arms, looked at her hands and checked her head for any injury. Luckily enough, I believe she had managed to avoid hitting her head because it was held up whilst she was rolling down. She was adamant she was fine but she was holding her hand up to her chest. When they looked at her hand they saw she had a small amount of skin scrapped off which was obviously causing her discomfort. My mum had a drink, stood up and the staff advised us to seek medical help if she became unwell later on and to keep a close eye on her. I was amazed that she seemed mostly unhurt and was so relieved that she didn't need another hospital visit. However, I was almost certain that she was playing down any pain she had and knew that rolling down an escalator had to have left its mark on my mum's body somewhere. There was no way she fell down in the manner she did and came out of it unharmed. My dad said he would give her a good check over once he had got her home. Later that day he phoned me with the reality of my mum's fall and sent me an email with the pictures of her bruised body. I knew that a fall like that would have left its mark, but I was just glad that apart from the bruises, my mum seemed OK. It's so hard because we tried our best to look after her and protect her but it's impossible to prevent all accidents. As her Alzheimer's was getting worse, the more upsetting it was to see her upset or in pain because she was suffering enough already. I just wanted to wrap her in bubble wrap and keep her from any potential hazards.

As things were getting tougher my dad informed me that I should apply for carers allowance. We were not aware of the carers allowance initially but once it was brought to light we thought it was worthwhile applying for it. He told me to apply for it because he believed that I deserved it and I also spent such a huge amount of time with my mum that I was a full time career alongside my dad. The only difference was that I didn't live with her but that didn't matter. Once the carers allowance was put into place, and it took a while, I received it for the short while I was caring for my mum full time. I received a small back dated payment but most of the time I was caring for my mum I couldn't prove my income as I was not the best at keeping my weekly payslips. Or whilst on maternity leave I sometimes received just over the value I could earn to claim the allowance. To be honest the hassle I had and for the short period of time I received the allowance it wasn't worthwhile for me. It just added to my stress and my list of things to do. However, my advice to anybody is if you are eligible to claim carers allowance, then do it as soon as possible. I missed out on months of the payment. This also applies to the PIP payment or any other disability payment. We were told to apply for PIP by the social worker and my mum did receive this but again it wasn't long before it was taken off her to help fund for her care a few months down the line. The person you're caring for has to be in receipt of their benefit before you can apply for your carers allowance, so don't delay. I also applied for a reduction in council tax and a disability badge for the car. The badge was great for us because my mum loved to wander and her lack of awareness meant she was always in danger of walking onto a road or an oncoming car. In a disability parking space you have less distance to travel and therefore smaller chance of anything bad happening. Also it allowed for room to assist my mum getting in and out of the car as this was something she couldn't really do on her own.

After months of coping mostly on our own my dad and I were informed that the carers were going to start. It was explained that my dad would have a carer go in every morning for an hour between 8a.m. and 8.30a.m. as that was roughly the time my mum would get out of bed, and somebody would also go in to clean on a Monday, Wednesday and Friday for an hour. He was sceptical about this help being offered because I think he was struggling to see any positives when things were just getting worse every day. The first morning the carer came, she got my mum out of bed, dressed and washed, teeth brushed and all sorted for her morning. I went round that morning as my dad wanted me to be there to answer any questions the carer had, and probably just to make himself feel a bit more comfortable. He is an awkward character like me and having someone go into his home in his private space wasn't something he would allow if he didn't need to. She was polite, patient and asked several questions regarding my mum so that she had a better understanding of the situation. Once everything was done for my mum, my dad said the carer could go home. As long as she was washed, teeth cleaned, dressed and hair dried my dad didn't mind how long it took, he would just tell the carer to go home.

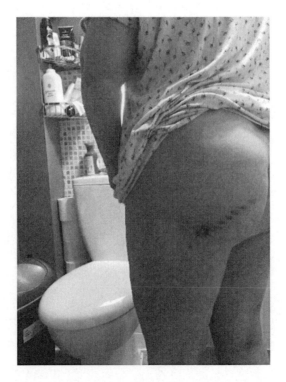

The allocated time slot was irrelevant and most days the carer was in and out within 20–30 minutes.

It wasn't long before my dad's sceptical attitude was proven right when the following week the carers were either late, no shows or not the most experienced dementia carer. He had a different carer showing up each morning and he wasn't impressed about that because my mum was having to get used to a different person showering her each morning. Stability is what my mum needed, not uncertainty. Some mornings they were showing up at 8.30a.m. and other mornings 9.30a.m. My dad would sometimes get a call after 9.30a.m. asking where he was because the carer was outside the house. He explained that he was told the carers would be there between 8.00a.m. and 8.30a.m. and he couldn't hang around waiting. When my mum woke up she wanted to get dressed and go out for breakfast, he couldn't leave her sat in a soiled or wet nappy and not get her dressed. Some days the carers just didn't show and when I rang the agency they explained that they hadn't actually sorted a permanent carer so they were basically just giving us whoever was available and couldn't promise us a time. This wasn't good enough for my dad, he is very much regimented and organised when it comes to routines. His army days have ensured he is always bound by times and structures. The caring system put into place at the moment was causing more disruption and anger for my dad and it wasn't worthwhile.

However, a few weeks later a routine and regular carer was finally put into place. She came in every morning and sorted my mum out whilst my dad waited downstairs and she became a known face to her. She also came in to do the cleaning 3 times a week and would make her a cup of tea and have a chat. Finally, the carer coming in was doing what was expected, and had lifted some of the stress off my dad. The carer coming in was friendly and genuinely caring. She brought my parent's gifts of luck that she had made herself and helped us out however she could. My mum found it quite amusing when she was showered in the morning, she would talk in the third person and laugh, 'she's getting showered and she has to put her arms up, and she can do it herself.' My dad would make light of the situation to her and say that she was lucky she had someone washing her. He used the term maid rather than carer to her when talking about it and said he didn't have the luxury of a maid. When my mum asked me if she washed me too I would just say yes and we would laugh about it. The care in place made us feel like we had taken 2 steps forward, it made things easier for my dad in the morning and his house was cleaned which eased the pressure off me. However, the Alzheimer's had other plans and pulled us 5 steps backwards once again.

The Fine Line Between Love and Hate

My mum was slowly declining before our eyes, and this time it was the mental decline that was going to slowly shatter our home life. Every day she was getting quieter with my dad and not making much conversation with him. She would mutter things under her breath if my dad went near her and became very cold and distant. She didn't like it when he cuddled her or kissed her like he always had and she wasn't appreciating any help he was trying to offer. Instead of asking for help or accepting help she was trying to do simple tasks by herself with not much luck. I had never seen my mum like this before. She had thrown the odd accusation or had an off day with us all but she never rejected my dad's love and affection. It was their bond that kept us all going strong. This was one of the hardest declines for my dad because he just wanted the wife he had known and loved for most of his life. He really struggled and his heart broke over and over again when she pushed him away. My mum began calling my dad names and she wanted to go out without him all the time. When I was available I would go round and take her out to give them both the break they needed but that wasn't always possible.

By this time I was off maternity leave and back at work. I had reduced my hours and was only working 2 evenings a week, but even this proved too much. After only being back for 1 week I received a call off my dad saying my mum kept trying to walk out of the house and she wanted me. He said she was pushing him out of the way and was being really hateful towards him. I said for him not to worry and I would be home as soon as I could. I cleared it with the ladies I worked with and left work. When I got to my parent's house my mum was sat in a room away from my dad and she was relieved to see me. She was saying all sorts of nonsense about my dad and not making any sense. She said he was a baby and he wore nappies because his mum always treated him like a baby. She described his mum as a nice lady and she was called Christine. Firstly, my dad's mum isn't called Christine and he definitely does not wear nappies (well at least I don't think he does 😊). She was going on and on about how my dad was a baby and that he didn't wear proper clothes. She spoke about how he couldn't look after himself and eventually she explained how she couldn't live in the same house as him. I took this statement with a pinch of salt and just hoped she was having one of those days that would be forgotten about the next day. I took her out in the car to the shop just to put a bit of space between my parents and to hopefully divert my mum's attention onto something else. Once we got back I got her sorted for bed and she went to sleep. We didn't know what the morning would have in store for us but we had to take each and every day as it came because predictable is one thing Alzheimer's is not.

The next few weeks were difficult, my mum was still being very withdrawn with my dad and I received numerous calls from my dad whilst I was at work. It was never any question that I was going to leave work if he called me for help because family was my priority, not work. I didn't feel great about having to leave work because I was paid to work but if my dad was calling me for help then it was important and I couldn't ignore that. If I didn't get a call whilst at work then I would go round to my parents straight after and get my mum dressed for bed, put her nappy on and do her teeth. This again just relieved some pressures off my dad, especially as she wasn't overjoyed to have him around anyway. The day she became un-cooperative with my dad I gave him the reassurance that every evening I would go round their house and get my mum ready for bed. Even when I had plans at my friend Kerry's house who lived a few minutes away from my parents I stuck by my promise. I set an alarm on my phone and when it was my mum's bedtime I ran round to their house, got my mum sorted and into bed and then went back to Kerry's. I knew how much me doing this helped my dad and I didn't want to let him down if I didn't need to. This was on top of taking her out, taking dinners round, sitting with her on a Saturday afternoon so that he could enjoy some time with his friend, collecting medications and going to each and every appointment and meeting regarding her welfare, etc. It did sometimes feel like a mammoth task and it consumed my life. My family time at home was limited but it really was the least I could do for my dad because I knew he had no escape. I could go home and get away for a few hours from the heartbreak and hard work but my dad couldn't, he lived with it. We had nobody else and my dad has said numerous times that without me helping he wouldn't have coped. Trying to keep my dad strong has kept me going strong. My mum's friend Elaine also helped on a few occasions whilst I was on my way home from work if my dad was struggling. I knew this couldn't continue because my dad was my mum's carer and if she didn't want him near her then that was going to make things incredibly difficult for them both. I knew it wasn't her fault it was the Alzheimer's but I had to keep reminding myself that so that I didn't resent her for the pain she was causing my dad.

It wasn't long before I got quite an agitated call from my dad and everything was getting rapidly worse. He frantically explained that my mum had been trying to walk out of the house all afternoon and she wasn't happy when he was trying to stop her. He then said she had walked out and walked off before he had chance to see what direction she had gone in. I could tell by his voice that his patience was wearing thin and he was starting to feel bitter towards my mum because of how she was treating him. He was also obviously concerned and upset by the whole situation. I told him I would get in my car and keep my eyes peeled for her. I picked Charlotte up and got into the car as quickly as I could. As I was driving the 2 minutes to my parent's house I was looking down every side road to make sure my mum wasn't wandering and then I got onto their estate. I kept looking down every road until I eventually spotted her about 50 metres away from her house. She was standing still and just looked really lost and confused, so I rang my dad to let him know she was safe. I then drove the car towards her, pulled up and got out. I asked her what she was doing and she just looked more confused and I asked her if she wanted to get into my car. She replied, 'yes,' and I took her home. As we went inside she made it very clear she wasn't happy about being back home. She said she didn't want to live with "him" anymore and I could see that this behaviour wasn't going to just stop anytime soon. She was name calling and adamant my dad wasn't to go anywhere near her.

My dad and I both knew that this couldn't continue, my mum was in danger going out of the house on her own. Due to the breakdown between them there was no way my dad could prevent her from walking out of the house if that was what she wanted to do. I couldn't be round their house all the time and we had tried our best so we decided the only option was to ring the social worker and explain the situation. She advised us that she would come out and assess what was happening. When the social worker arrived she had a mental health nurse with her who introduced herself. They sat down with my mum and asked her how she was and what was going on. She didn't try and hide the dislike of my dad and she just kept saying she couldn't stay there with him. When questioned about her walking out of the house my mum didn't see the issue. That was one of the hardest things to deal with because she thought she was fine and should be able to go out on her own. However, we knew differently and recognised that she could end up lost or in danger. She would tell us she wanted to go to the bingo over the road but there was no bingo over the road. It didn't matter how many times I said that bingo was in town which was far away, she didn't believe me. She was adamant all her thoughts and visions were correct and nobody was going to tell her differently. My mum muttered a few incoherent sentences about my dad to the social worker and made it clear she couldn't stay in the house with him. Whilst explaining why she was upset with my dad, most of which didn't make sense, my mum exclaimed she hated him. When questioned who she hated, she pointed to the stairs where my dad was sitting and said in a stern cranky voice, 'him.'

The social worker and colleague could see that there was a breakdown and it was going to cause issues and they said those words that we never wanted to hear even again, 'she needs to be sectioned.' They explained that my mum wasn't safe and she couldn't be kept in and watched at all times. They were worried that she would walk out of the house and my dad's attempt at stopping her could cause more issues. My dad and I just looked at each other, with faces of disappointment but we were also both fully aware we had no other option. We couldn't help my mum if she didn't want us to. However there was no way we were allowing her to go into the same hospital as last time. My dad insisted she was put in somewhere different regardless of where was closer. The lady with the social worker agreed and said she would get back to us later that day regarding what was happening. So they left us to it, and I stayed at my dad's house until I needed to so that my mum didn't keep walking out.

Hours and hours passed and we heard nothing, I even tried the social worker's phone and couldn't get through, the wait was so unnerving. I was angry that I was told my mum was getting sectioned and they would get back to me and we had heard nothing. They said she was unsafe and yet they had just left us with no support and no knowledge about what was happening next. I decided to phone the crisis team and they said they didn't really know what was happening and if we needed help because things got worse to ring for an ambulance. Once again I felt incredibly let down and my dad was at the end of his tether. There was nothing more I could do so I just stayed with my parents until the late evening, got my mum ready for bed and then went home. The following day I went straight round and surprisingly my mum seemed slightly better and she wasn't being as distant and rude towards my dad. This didn't mean everything was great because it wasn't, it just wasn't as bad as the day before. We headed out for breakfast and carried on like every other day. As my dad and I had the entire night to think about the day before we both decided we didn't want my mum sectioned. This wasn't because we didn't think she needed it because deep down we knew she would probably revert back to walking out of the house and pushing my dad away again. We were scared, worried and pessimistic about the care she would receive and therefore we didn't want her going anywhere. I contacted the social worker and explained that my mum appeared better and we didn't want her sectioned. I also stated that we were not informed about what was happening and it wasn't really good enough. She said that the decision had been made and that I would receive a phone call in due course from the lady that was at the house the day before with her. A very short while later I got the call and she explained how they couldn't get a team together to section my mum the night before. However it was being done in a few hours because it had already been decided that my mum needed sectioning. I asked what it would mean if my dad and I had changed our mind and she specified that it was out of our control. So we decided to head home and wait to see what happened.

Not long after a team of professionals showed up at my parent's door. They all came in and had a chat with my mum and straight away it was obvious they were going ahead with the section. A lady went into the other room with my dad and discussed the decision with him further. She pointed out that my mum's relationship with him had broken down and he was the key person to hold everything together. She explained that if he couldn't stop her walking out of the house then it would only lead to my mum being sectioned anyway or worse. He was promised her medication would be looked into and hopefully something could be done to help with some of the symptoms she was experiencing. After a lengthy chat my dad was happy for them to proceed but he had one condition, she was not going to the hospital she stayed in the last time. It was agreed. The team rang around and eventually informed us that the nearest mental health hospital with space available was a 1-hour drive away. There was no other option unless she went into the same hospital as before, so we approved their decision. At this point my dad said he didn't want to be around for when my mum was taken away so he got into his car and drove to a local pub and waited for me to inform him when it was all done.

Everybody left apart from a mental health nurse who waited with me until the ambulance that had been arranged arrived. It was like déjà vu. I had the same knot in my stomach and the same questions about what the right thing to do was, spinning round and round in my head. I had a good chat with the mental health nurse about dementia and her job. She agreed when I expressed my concerns about how somebody that has dementia was sectioned in the exact same way somebody else without dementia experiencing a psychotic episode. I didn't agree with sectioning somebody with Alzheimer's and them being sent somewhere where the staff lack the understanding needed. About 20 minutes before the ambulance arrived my sister showed up and I couldn't help but be angry towards her. It seemed she always arrived when things got to the tip of the iceberg but she had no understanding of the huge amount of work, care and time required before things got to that point. I on the other hand, had spent the weekend walking the streets with my mum, sitting with her whilst my dad had some rest bite, waiting for health professionals and waiting for an ambulance.

The ambulance eventually arrived and I had once again packed my mum a bag. She was a lot less anxious this time but more upset. I was informed of what hospital she was being taken to and given phone numbers so that I could ring if I needed to. She started crying saying she didn't want to go but she didn't put up a fight. We said our goodbyes and my sister led her to the ambulance. Once again I was heartbroken not knowing what the hospital was like and not knowing what the outcome of the section would be once more.

Mental Health Hospital 2
History Repeated, Inadequately Treated, Feeling Defeated

The following day after my mum was sectioned I wasn't leaving a settling in period this time. I told my dad I was going to see her to make sure she was OK and not in the same situation as last time. He advised me to leave it a while but I had made up my mind and went anyway. I stopped at a shop and got my mum some fresh orange juice and some chocolate on the way. After the hour long drive I was relieved when I finally saw the hospital and pulled up into the car park, I hate driving on roads I don't know. I walked along to the mental health building, pressed the buzzer and it wasn't long before somebody came and let me in. As I got inside my stomach was doing somersaults because I knew if I didn't like what I saw I would probably have to just grin and bear it. I couldn't moan again about a hospital without very good reason because this was the second time she had now been sectioned and it was done for a good reason. I walked along a few corridors and saw some other patients. The first thing I noticed is that they were not all as old as the last hospital which definitely gave a different feel straight away. There wasn't a lot of room and it felt quite enclosed which I didn't like, there was less room than the other hospital. There were a few people sat on chairs talking to themselves, some were sleeping and I just imagined how bored they must have been with the lack of space. Then I saw my mum, she was frantically walking up and down the short space she had. She was muttering to herself and when she saw me she continued her muttering, asking if I was going out too and explaining that she was going out to the shop. Her face was flushed and sweaty and she was obviously getting very hot with all the walking she was doing. It was quite warm in the building and my mum was wearing a big thick jumper which wouldn't have been helping matters. Every time I stood in front of her to talk to her she continued to pace around me, she was obviously extremely agitated. She was happy to see me and did smile and talk to me, even if it was gibberish, but she was just on the move all the time.

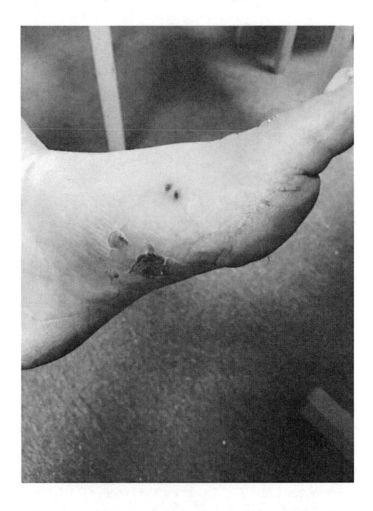

I eventually persuaded her to come to her room after being shown where it was by a member of staff. I sat her down on the bed and asked her if she felt hot because she looked very clammy and she told me she was. I looked at the selection of clothes I had packed for her and there wasn't any light or summer clothes. As it was winter I had packed jumpers and leggings and that was it. I was wearing a strap top as I like to feel unrestricted when driving long distances, so closed her bedroom door and swapped tops with her. I put on her big thick jumper that smelled of body odour and I gave my mum my strap top so she could get some air and cool down. I was a bit annoyed that she was just left sweating in a jumper all day, they could have called me and informed me to take some cooler clothes or just put her nightdress on in place of the jumper. I was so hot in her jumper there was no way I could have worn it for any length of time my mum had been. I sat my mum in a chair and gave her some of her chocolate and orange juice.

She was behaving so frantically and talking absolute nonsense. She was telling me about a baby down the street and she kept saying they had a baby, the baby was there soon and she couldn't believe they had a baby. She asked if I knew the baby and I questioned if she meant Charlotte and she said no. We had a couple of other really absurd conversations and I just said minimal responses and went along with what she was saying. In-between talking to me she was also talking to herself, making absolutely no sense what so ever. My mum then started to question why she had to stay there and I explained that she needed to get some help with her medication. She responded by saying, 'I am not mad you know, they think I'm mad but I'm not.' However she wasn't talking to me she was talking with her head facing to her left and laughing. Like she was talking to somebody I couldn't see. I used this opportunity to make a joke and ask her why she was talking to herself and explained that it did make her look mad and she just laughed.

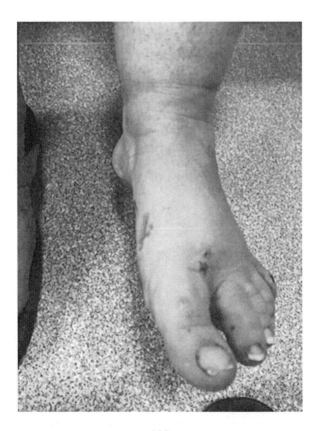

After a while my mum started complaining about her feet. She was wearing her fit flops that she usually found very comfy. She had always worn them and never had any problems with them before. I knelt down beneath her and proceeded to remove the fit flops from her feet. As I was taking them off I was disgusted, upset and annoyed by what I saw. Her skin was coming away with the footwear, it was stuck to them. She had wounds and blisters on her feet that looked so painful it saddened me to see, knowing she must have been so uncomfortable and yet she was just getting on with it. One of the wounds was so big it almost looked like a hole in her foot on the sole. I was so mad that she had been allowed to walk up and down all day allowing the blisters to get as bad as they were. Why weren't her fit flops changed to some anti slip socks, or the slippers I packed for her? The slippers were fluffy and would have been very warm but I would have much preferred my mum's feet to be hot and sweaty, than wounded and sore. I was so distressed by what I was seeing because once again she had been put into somebody else's care and she was worse off once more. I went and found a member of staff and showed them her feet and they explained that my mum did lots of walking up and down all day and she wasn't wearing suitable footwear. They asked me to bring in something more comfortable and I explained that I would come back up the following day with some open toed slippers and her trainers. I felt like I was treading on egg shells because I didn't want to upset the staff because they were going to be looking after my mum for the foreseeable, but I couldn't understand why her feet had been allowed to get that bad and why they weren't treating the wounds. I said my goodbyes and left the hospital feeling disappointed but knowing that I couldn't tell my dad, not after the negative experience at the last hospital. My dad was finding it really hard with my mum being sectioned so I didn't want to give him any reasons to worry.

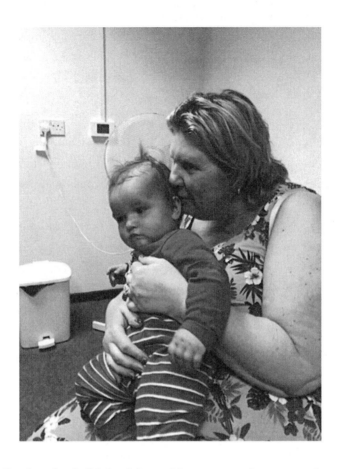

The following day I did the 1-hour drive once again to go and see my mum. I took Charlotte with me this time and also took my mum's slippers, trainers, some lighter clothing and a pack of chocolate twists. When I got to the main door I was informed that I would need to go into the family room as I had Charlotte with me and she wasn't allowed onto the main corridor with all the patients. They told me that they would go and get my mum and bring her to me. Whilst I waited in the room for her I could hear a commotion and it sounded like it involved her, so I stood up and opened the door. The staff were trying to get my mum to the room but she wasn't happy about them telling her where to go. She was shouting, 'get off me,' and 'don't touch me.' She was swearing and very agitated, the staff asked if I would be OK on my own with her. I said it would be fine because I knew her upset state was due to the situation she had been placed in and she would be happy to see a familiar face. When my mum saw me she was more obliging, and came into the family room. I had never seen her in such a frantic, anxious, upset and vulnerable way before. She was speaking so fast I couldn't catch most of what she was saying and once again she was sweating hot. She kept begging me for water and saying that she hadn't had a drink all day. She asked me why there was no water anywhere and told me that she wasn't allowed to have any. She kept repeating this over and over again every few minutes until I went and got a cup of water for her. She was smiling and talking to Charlotte and it was nice to see her calming down slightly. I gave my mum the slippers to put on her feet and saw that some cream had been put onto the wounds. I felt quite concerned whilst with her because once again it was quite clear to me that she was unbalanced and declining more whilst she was away from her home. When Alzheimer's was taking her away from me each and every day I didn't want anything speeding that process up. I was just building all the negatives in my head and the sense of guilt was rippling through my body once again. Why did we call the professionals when there was always that chance she would get sectioned again? I had to keep reminding myself that she was walking out of the house and it wasn't safe for her. She would be safer in the hospital where she couldn't leave. Wouldn't she?

After a few minutes of chatting and eating chocolate twists my mum raised her arms up into the air to have a stretch. As she lifted her arms I was horrified at what I thought I saw. I took a closer look and saw several small bruises all down her arm. I checked the other arm and that one wasn't quite as bad but it was also bruised. I questioned my mum about the bruises and she said she didn't know how they got there. I had a good look at both arms and to me they looked like finger marks, like she had been grabbed too hard. I was absolutely fuming to the point where I wanted to walk out with my mum and take her home and also burst into tears at the same time. I didn't know how those bruises got there and I never will know but they looked like grab marks to me. She had never had bruises like that on her arms before whilst she was cared for by us, so why were they there now? I decided I had seen enough and went to find a member of staff to ask about the bruises. She was unsympathetic, uncaring and not really interested. The explanation I was given was that my mum must have done them herself, her nails were quite long and that was probably the cause! I argued that the bruises didn't look like nail marks but they looked like grip marks and she just brushed my remark aside and was insistent my mum had caused the bruises herself. She said I needed to bring nail scissors in and cut her nails so that it didn't happen again and I agreed to bring nail scissors in as her nails were long.

However, I did not agree that this was the cause of the bruising. I felt so upset, alone and confused.

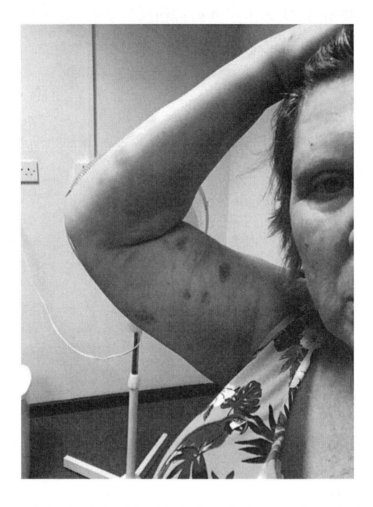

Once again I felt ashamed that I had left her in the care of somebody else and she was in a worse state than when she went in. She was talking nonsense, she wasn't eating the meals she was given, she was hot and sweaty, her feet were in a disgusting state and she was covered in bruises. I was starting to think that mental health hospitals were not the right place for Alzheimer's patients at all. They lack in all the real care required and once again I didn't know what to do or where to turn. I started thinking about how it would be if my mum moved in with me if she didn't want to be in the house with my dad. I knew it wasn't feasible with the children to look after too but I was so angry and upset that at that moment in time I would have done anything to help. I needed to get some advice and quickly so I said goodbye and left the building.

As soon as I got out of the hospital I rang my aunty Sue, who I had sent pictures of the bruised arms and blistered feet to a few minutes before. She answered the phone and without no hesitation told me that my mum needed to be at home. She said that my she looked unwell and needed to be cared for at home, and she was absolutely disgusted by the bruises. She agreed with me that there was no way my mum was bruising the underside of her arms herself and that it looked like she had been grabbed quite forcefully. I told my aunty that I didn't know what to do about my dad, should I tell him or not and she said he would want to know. I agreed that he would want to know but I also knew that he was going to be beyond angry and he would not rest unless something was done about it. We decided I would tell my dad when I got home and then we would do what we could to get answers. My aunty asked me for the phone number of the ward my mum was on so she could phone up and find out what was going on, and she rang them. After a few minutes she rang me back and told me that the lady wasn't too interested. She had told her that my mum had probably done the bruises herself and I agreed with that explanation. I couldn't actually believe what I was hearing, I did not agree with that at all. I told my aunty that I questioned the lady and said I would bring nail clippers in but I did not agree that the bruises were caused by my mum's nails. I was fuming that they were putting words into my mouth and that they took my shyness and non-argumentative attitude as an admittance of something I did not agree with. I felt I made it clear enough I didn't agree the bruises were done by my mum and that they looked like grab marks. This was the final straw for me. I got straight off the phone to my aunty and on the phone to the social worker.

I knew I sounded like a broken record but I explained to her that my mum was not staying in that hospital. I was outraged that I had even allowed it to happen and it was not ever going to happen again. I went on to explain what had happened and that I strongly disagreed that my mum should be in hospital, she needed care and attention. I told the social worker that if she needed to be anywhere then she needed a care home with activities and more space not a hospital. She needed trained carers that ensured she was clean, healthy, eating, drinking and getting help with all the tasks she couldn't complete herself. My plan was to get her out of the hospital and back home with some extra care put into place. I explained that if a career came to look after my mum for more than 1 hour a day then maybe it would keep her mind active and busy. I said that maybe we could look into respite for her a few times a week. I wanted to go down the correct route for my mum's care and that didn't include anymore hospital stays. I was told to leave it with her and she would get back to me.

After a few days I was informed that my mum would be having a small review to see how things were going so I said I would attend too. That morning my dad had Charlotte for me so that I didn't have the added pressure of looking after her. My dad didn't want to attend the review because he was so heated about the situation so far he thought it best he stayed away. When I got to the hospital I was taken to my mum and we waited to be called into the review. She was still very apprehensive and pacing the floor muttering to herself. There was definitely no sign of any improvement, only decline. Once we got called in to the review we took a seat in a room with several other medical professionals. I was anxious and feeling under pressure once again. They all introduced themselves and explained that we were there to see how things were going. They asked my mum how she was and she just rambled on about how her mum was only up the road. She made no sense what so ever and it was quite obvious she was unsure what was happening and she was very uneasy. She got a bit upset which in turn made my eyes fill up because I hated seeing her so distressed. I just kept thinking that she must have been so confused about what was happening and she couldn't even express that to us, which must have made it even harder for her. The consultant was a lady and she was such a good listener and really empathetic. I explained to her how I was concerned about my mum's welfare because she was declining and obviously very destressed. I also expressed my concern about her feet and the state they had got into and the bruises on her arms. I obviously couldn't point fingers but I did stress that I felt they looked like grab marks, and they insisted they hadn't used any force with my her because she was always so compliant. However I felt that it didn't necessarily mean the bruises weren't caused by a firm grip because my mum was submissive, they could have been caused by lifting her up and using too much force. They tried to reassure me by advising me that my mum would have a body map done so that any marks or bruises would be marked down on paper and also that she would be regularly monitored throughout the day. I agreed with this and they said we would have another review in a week's time and see how things were going. They were using the medication that my mum was prescribed previously to be used as and when needed. It was supposed to calm her and they said that hopefully she would be a bit more settled. Although they had put things in place and tried to reassure me, I didn't have much faith in other people caring for her especially after what I had seen already. I was still going to push to get her home and would never accept her going into a hospital again. We needed a different route if the time arose again.

The week passed very quickly and I visited my mum about 3 times in that week. I couldn't go every day because it was such a long drive but I had to keep a close eye on what was happening and wanted her to know she wasn't on her own. I didn't enjoy going and I found it upsetting every time I had to leave. I didn't feel like my mum was improving at all during the week and I was ready to fight to get her back home when it was time for the review. I got Shaun to book the Monday off so that I didn't need to worry about the kids and I could attend the review on my own. I spoke to my dad and he made it very clear he couldn't face the review with me this time and I needed to do it on my own, he was so angry that he didn't feel it was right he be in there in case he made the situation worse. He told me to make sure I got my mum out of that hospital, if they didn't let her out I was supposed to tell them he would break her out if he had to, and that he couldn't cope without her. With this in mind I drove back to the hospital for the review with a huge amount of pressure on my shoulders but also the burning fire needed to get her back where she needed to be. This review was set out the same as last time but my mum was absent this time. They opened up by explaining how my mum was doing well and she was very compliant with the rules and her medications. They expressed that it hadn't been very long and they felt some more time would benefit her. However I could see the consultant was also very willing to listen to what I had to say. It was another really emotional moment, and I couldn't fight back the tears whilst talking regardless of how hard I tried. I described how my mum was declining every day she was away from home, how she was getting really anxious and needed 24-hour care by people that knew how to care for her properly. I spoke passionately about how I felt my mum was not needing a mental health hospital but understanding, time and love. I said my dad was falling apart without her by his side even though she was rejecting him and we knew we needed extra support and care coming in to enable her to stay at home for as long as we could manage. I also opened up and sadly uttered that I knew my mum was rapidly declining and it wouldn't be long before she needed a home but we wanted every day that we could with her at home. Every single day had become so precious and it was such a struggle having her an hour away without traffic. The consultant looked at her team and she looked at me with sympathetic and understanding eyes. I think she may have even had a tear in her eye when she told me that she would allow my mum home with the permission of my dad as he was living with her. I knew from the first review that the consultant was considerate and compassionate and she had proven that to me. She backed up her decision by explaining how my mum was happily taking her medication and didn't once need restraining. I was so happy and thanked all the staff with an appreciative smile. They rang my dad off my mobile to see how he felt about my mum being allowed home and of course he was over the moon. I knew from that moment on we needed to be more prepared for what the future held. I didn't want her to ever have to be sectioned ever again.

We got to the car and it became so apparent the section had a huge knock-on effect with my mum. She was unable to get into the car and kept getting her feet confused. Once we eventually got into the car I took her to a MacDonald's drive through and got her a drink and a cheeseburger as she said she was starving. She was trying to eat the wrapper of the burger and was tipping the coke up to her lips ignoring the straw and the lid. I had to keep placing the straw in her mouth and reminding her to not tip the drink. It was so sad because I felt like we had aggravated the Alzheimer's by placing my mum somewhere she didn't know and increased her anxiety levels. I just hoped that once she got settled at home she would be more relaxed and things could plod on like they were before. She greeted my dad at home with a hug and a smile which was great considering how things were left and my dad turned to me and said, 'Your mum is not going anywhere like that ever again,' and I was in full agreement.

The Inevitable Final Breakdown

My dad and I were fully aware that it wasn't going to be easy having Mum back at home again, and we expected some days to be worse than others. We were prepared to have days where we struggled and my dad had come to terms with the possibility that my mum may dislike him some days. We both realised that my mum being in hospital and not getting the care she needed was far more distressing than having her at home. We just wanted what was best for her because that was what she deserved. However, once we got home we spoke to the social worker and asked for extra care to be put into place. We were hoping for an extra hour each day and possibly even some respite on certain days. We were informed by the social worker that due to my mum being sectioned for the second time she now was entitled to free aftercare. Section 117 of the Mental Health Act sets out that Local Authorities have to provide aftercare to certain detained patients once they have been released from hospital. The aftercare should only stop if and when it is no longer needed to stay well. In my mum's case it was explained that she would never become better as Alzheimer's gets worse and therefore the aftercare would always be relevant to her. This made life a little easier because we could put the help into place that she needed without worrying. We knew that although we asked for extra care, it wouldn't happen overnight. It took quite a few weeks to put into place last time so we expected the same this time. We just hoped we could pull together and things didn't get any worse.

I knew we needed to be more prepared this time round and was fully aware that if the time came, and we weren't able to care for my mum, then we would need to have an idea of the care home we wanted her to be placed into. It was either that or a hospital and that was not an option again. Therefore I spoke to the social worker and she gave me a list of 3 homes to have a look around. One was not in our local area and was about a 40-minute drive when the traffic was good, and the other two were both less than 10 minutes away. So one weekend I decided to go and have a look around the homes so I could get an idea of what they were like, I have never really been in a care home so didn't know what to expect.

The first home I went to visit was the closest. I was so nervous and felt sick to my stomach, I couldn't actually quite believe I was looking for a new home for my mum. I had to be able to imagine myself visiting this place daily and I also needed it to be somewhere I could take my children to see their nanny. I felt sad that it was only 16 months since my mum was diagnosed and I was already looking at care homes. When I pulled up the home looked very modern and stylish from the outside. I walked up to the main door and pressed the buzzer, I was greeted by a member of staff. They explained they would come and let me in and show me round. As I walked inside I thought it looked clean and quite open, there was lots of windows and lights. This was important because of my mum's claustrophobia. I saw a sensory room, the dining room and a lovely conservatory type room. It was nice and the surrounding garden was also pleasant. When I passed the dining room it was lunch time and the residents were eating their meal. I couldn't help but feel sad when I saw them and they all looked old. I just found it impossible to imagine my mum sat with them when most of them were old enough to be her parents and also a lot of them looked less mobile than she was. I knew I had to try and forget about this because it wouldn't matter where I visited there was always going to be more old people because Alzheimer's generally effects older people. There was nothing I could do about that, but it was just so difficult to place her somewhere that I felt she was too young for. I was informed of some activities that were put on for the residents but they didn't sound like they would be my mum's cup of tea. They were planned with all the older residents in mind. With that said it was a pleasant home and I could see her living there if I really had to. The home was clean and modern but I felt it lacked the homely feel. I knew that no home was going to make me feel like I was making a positive choice and I wasn't going to feel 100% about anywhere, or at least that was what I thought.

I said thank you to the staff member that showed me round and headed to the second home on my list that was local. On the way I reflected on what was happening, I broke down in tears and reality hit me. My mum was only 55 and I was choosing her care home. Even though she had been diagnosed with Alzheimer's I didn't expect to be at this stage already. I just couldn't imagine a permanent life without her at home by my dad's side like she always had been. As I pulled up to the next home I was even more impressed than before. This home looked inviting, well looked after and modern. There were fresh summer flowers planted on the front, it was well maintained and I could see pretty fairly lights running across the building. I walked through the main door and was hit with a lovely welcoming floral scent, it was so nice I was tempted to ask what they were using so that I could have it in my home. It would make a change from the wet dog, dirty nappies and sweaty husband scent my home normally presented. I was let into the main foyer through the security locked door and walked to the main reception desk to explain that I wanted to have a look around. The lady on the desk asked if I had an appointment and I said I didn't, but she stopped what she was doing and said she would show me around the home.

The foyer was clean, stylish and felt more like walking into a hotel than a care home. There were vases filled with fresh flowers that might sound simple but gave the homely feel I was looking for. I was impressed already, but even more impressed when I turned to my left and saw a hairdressing and beauty salon. I asked if that was for the residents and the receptionist told me that a hairdresser came in during the week to do their hair. I was so pleased because it was so important for me to keep my mum doing the things she loved, getting her hair and nails done, keep her looking as nice as she always did. I felt like I had walked into a small society with everything they needed under the one roof. There was even a large fish tank which was just another thing that was proof to me that this home was happy to maintain a high-quality lifestyle. I was told about the three different floors and what they were for and then I was showed around. The biggest difference I noticed straight away from how I imagined a care home to be was the carpets laid throughout. Carpets are warm, homely and comfortable, but they are also hard to keep clean. However these carpets were very well maintained and I couldn't smell a single foul smell, they were obviously very well looked after. Straight away I was getting the feeling that this home didn't just go for easy options and what would make their life easier or cheaper but they did what was the best for the residents. I walked up the corridor and looked into each room as I passed, they were all individual and were very spacious. Some had huge comfy chairs, pictures all over the wall, brightly coloured curtains, each and every one was different. I was shown inside a room, it was so open and also came with an en-suite. There was so much space to make the room personal to the individual. I was told by the receptionist that the rooms were the homes of the people staying in them and therefore anything could be done with them. They could be decorated, furniture added and pictures added to the walls. This was music to my ears because if my mum was in a home I would want to make it suit her tastes and age. Make it as modern and stylish as my mum's homes have always been throughout her life with my dad. I was shown a cinema room, a lounge and dining area and also a brasserie. A sensory room, a woodland relaxing room, a balcony area, a music room and another dining room. Each and every room was unique, contemporary and trendy. It was lovely to see that nothing was decorated like an old people's home, it was just the way you would expect a nice hotel to be. The woodland room was absolutely beautiful and the first thing that really caught my eye were the double doors opening onto the chic and relaxing balcony. Again, a very important factor for me when choosing somewhere for my mum was the space she would have to roam and the open space she would have access too. I loved the fact she could wander outside for fresh air anytime she desired because this would be very important for my mum's mental state and anxiety. The balcony contained some modern garden furniture, surrounded by beautiful hanging baskets and flower pots and the sun was gleaming right onto it. It really was stunning. Every little fine detail was what made this home exceptional, the fresh flowers in vases on the dining room tables, the memory boxes outside each and every room with memorable pictures for the residents, the stylishly decorated corridor walls with canvases, and the fresh, fragranced scent of the entire building. I was shown the menu for the week and it included all homemade nutritious dishes including the most delicious puddings for dessert. Food ranged from sandwiches and homemade soups to salmon en croute with mash and vegetables. I was blown away by the time, effort and money that had obviously been put into this home, it was just fantastic in every way.

On the way back towards the main reception we went to have a look at the garden. I didn't think I could be impressed anymore but oh my, I was wrong. The garden was absolutely huge and very well kept. It had huge marquees set up that I was informed were used for events which were very frequent in the summer, and a variety of garden furniture. There was a path that circulated round the garden which was good for the residents that were not as mobile and also grass, shrubs and plants. The garden was massive and so beautiful to look at, the sort of garden we all want in our own homes. I had seen more than enough and was extremely impressed. The staff that I did see whilst looking around were friendly and attentive with the residents, the receptionist was friendly, empathetic and showed an interest when asking about my mum and the

Alzheimer's and the cleaners were chatting and involved with the residents. It really did feel like one big family and I was blown away by the quality of this home. Just before I left I was shown a dining room near the main reception and was informed that they held meals for relatives of residents and it just needed to be booked in advance. It was so stylish and tasteful just like the rest of the home. I also saw a blackboard that detailed all the activities that were being put on for the residents for the week. The receptionist explained that activities included things like, afternoon tea, bingo, singers and musicians, shows, days out, creativity, pub nights and exercise classes. I was astounded by the vast array of activities that had so much effort put into them. It was lovely to see that all the activities were not just for old people and that the residents had more of a life than I did. I thanked the receptionist and gave her my details. As I left the home I had a warm pleasing feeling inside of me that I didn't ever think I would get from looking around a care home. This place was amazing and I couldn't imagine any place better when the time came for my mum to go into care. Before I got into my car I turned round and looked back once more and saw an advertising banner that said, 'Alderwood Care Home: Rated Outstanding,' and this it most certainly was. I couldn't wait to tell my dad all about it and how perfect it would be for my mum in the future.

It was only about a week of my mum being out of hospital and things were getting tougher and tougher. I felt apprehensive about what was going to happen next all the time. She was getting harder to please and a lot more eager to leave the house on her own. She wanted to go to the sports hall over the road, to the bingo down the street or just for a walk. Unbeknown to my mum there wasn't a sports hall or bingo nearby and the streets she had lived on for 20 years, were no longer familiar to her. She started becoming more agitated and was constantly pacing the floors of the house like a lion trapped in captivity. The days were getting tougher, longer and more consuming than ever. Then we were back to where we were a few weeks ago and my mum started becoming agitated with my dad again. She was trying to walk out of the house every day and it became normal to have to follow her on a short walk to nowhere at least once a day. Our patience was wearing thin and I rang the social worker to chase up the extra help or respite. It still wasn't ready to be put into place and I expressed to her the urgency of the situation. I made it clear that my mum was not being sectioned again but that things were getting rapidly worse. Once again we were waiting for paperwork to be done before the care or respite could happen. I was glad that I had looked around a few care homes but we were just holding out hope that we could keep her at home for a little while longer. We were praying we could endure the wait but I think deep down we knew that my mum wasn't happy at home and neither were we. She was frustrated when she wasn't allowed out of the house on her own or was told what to do and we were getting frustrated with having to upset her by not allowing her the freedom she wanted. I felt like I was looking after a baby that had just learnt to walk because the minute I took my eyes off her, she was walking off in another direction. I got numerous calls from my dad saying he needed my help because she wanted to go out of the house without him and I would have to take her to a shop just to take her mind off the situation. I knew it wasn't going to be long before something had to give because we were all stressed and finding it difficult including my mum.

Then came the day that was to change the shape of our lives forever. My dad couldn't cope with the heartache and grief at losing the connection he had always had with my mum for the past 40 years. I was surprised that he persevered for as long as he did because her pushing him away was killing him inside and caring for her was consuming our lives entirely. One morning I got a call and it was my dad, he sounded really distressed. He explained to me through words of anguish that he couldn't do it anymore. He said he needed to get away and my mum needed to go into care because he felt like his heart was being ripped out on a daily basis. I totally agreed with my dad because it was getting to the point where it was too much for me too. My dad told me he was going to Manchester for a few days and that he wanted me and my sister between us to take care of my mum until she was placed in to the right care home. It was such a hard decision for my dad to make and a difficult decision for me to agree with. She needed more space, more freedom and not to be told that she couldn't walk out of the door of the house that she had walked out for many years before on her own without a problem. I was saddened but also not surprised, we couldn't offer my mum what she needed anymore and it wasn't fair on any of us.

My dad left for Manchester instantly and he knew I would sort everything out and do my best by my mum. I rang my sister and told her that my dad couldn't cope and he had gone away for a few days and that we needed to get care put into place. I explained to her that I was struggling and I needed her help this time. I didn't want to be placing my mum into a permanent home on my own if I didn't have to. We decided between us as that my sister would stay at mine with all the children except Tommy and he would stay at my mum's with Shaun and I. That way when Shaun left for work at 6a.m. my sister was home for the children, I could drop Tommy at school because it was only round the corner and my mum wasn't left on her own. Also I felt she would be less likely to have another breakdown if I stayed with her at night rather than my sister. Once the school drops were done my sister joined me and we cared for my mum together. I rang the social worker and explained that we no longer needed extra help but we needed a care home as soon as possible. When I informed her that my dad had gone to Manchester as he couldn't cope she knew it was a matter of urgency and said she would call me back. I decided to ring Alderwood myself and see if there was any chance my mum could go their because I had my heart set on that place, however I was distraught to hear that they had no spaces available and they had a waiting list. This completely crushed the plan I had all set out in my head, I didn't really think about spaces being unavailable and I stupidly just thought I chose a home and my mum went in there.

The social worker rang me back and informed me that the care home that was about 40 minutes away had a space for my mum. She said it specialised in dementia and it had a decent reputation for being a good home. This wasn't going to be a permanent place for my mum but just a temporary fix before my mum could be placed somewhere closer. She told me to ring her back when I had made a decision to let her know. I didn't actually go and have a look around this home because of the distance but I knew if the social worker was telling me it was good, then it was, and that would have to do for now. We had no other option and I needed to sort something before we ended up in a situation where we had no choice where she went. I had a look online and although I was fully aware everything always looks so much better on the internet than in reality, it did look acceptable for now. I rang my aunty Sue and she agreed that if it was OK then we needed to take it because we didn't have many more options. I then rang the social worker and told her we would like to go ahead with the move to the home. She advised me that an assessment needed to be done first by somebody from the home but as time was passing this would need to be sorted the following day. My sister and I both decided that we would have to ring in work and explain we wouldn't be in because we were not aware of when my mum would be going into the home at this point. We just explained we would keep them updated.

The evening went relatively well considering the last time my mum was without my dad in the evening she became agitated and aggressive. The following morning I received a call from the social worker and she explained that the assessment could be done later on that day but she didn't know for sure. So we carried on with the day as normal, we took my mum out and then came home. We spent a lot of time sat on sun loungers out of the front of the house as she kept wanting to stand outside the front door. Luckily it was a lovely sunny day so we just went with the flow and tried to keep her as happy as we could. We had to follow her on a few walks around the estate but again we just persevered with keeping everything satisfactory for her. The day passed by and we had no word about the assessment so just assumed it wasn't happening. It was a tough day having to basically be on full alert at all times, it felt like we were taking in turns to be a life guard at a swimming pool. We couldn't take our eyes of our mum for more than a second because she would be up from her chair and walking off again. The following morning we were having breakfast in Costa when I got a call to inform me the lady that would be doing the assessment was outside my mum's house. So we got into the car as quickly as possible and drove back to her house and met the lady on the front.

As we invited her in my mum's anxiety levels started increasing straight away. She started questioning why she was there and didn't want to sit down. So my sister kept an eye on her whilst I sat down and had a chat with the lady. She told me all about the home and then asked me about my mum. She went through some paperwork and I had to answer quite a few questions and that was it, the assessment was complete. She didn't inform me whether the assessment had been successful because she said she had to take it back and go through it and then I would be informed later that day. I was so nervous because if it didn't to plan, then what? I could not have my mum placed just anywhere and I wouldn't allow that to happen, but we also couldn't go on the way we were. The hours passed by and I heard nothing. I got on the phone to social worker again and she had heard nothing so we just waited. The day continued until eventually it was the evening and we still had no news, so I went to bed and hoped that tomorrow would be the day.

That next morning I got a call from the social worker to explain that my mum had passed the assessment and we were just waiting for the paperwork to be finalised and then she could go into the home. However I couldn't be given a specific time or even a day so again it was just a waiting game. I was relieved to know the assessment was passed but still nervous because until my mum was actually in the home I felt anything could happen before then. The day was passing on and I kept pushing for a time because we had no idea what was happening and our lives had been well and truly turned upside down. Shaun was sleeping on a couch and so was Tommy and my sister was staying at my house with my baby and other daughter. We spent our days trying to keep my mum calm and compliant and that left not much time for anything else. A few hours later I got a call to say she could go into the home. I felt a mixture of happiness, sorrow and relief. I explained that I would drive her there myself with my sister and we would arrive there in a few hours so that we could leave all the children with Shaun once he was home from work. I went upstairs in my mum's bedroom and packed a few things she would need. This time wasn't like the others because although she was only temporarily going into this home, I knew she wouldn't be coming back to her own home again. Tears fell as I packed her essentials and a few photos into a bag. I felt relief after a stressful and hard few months, but I felt like I had given up on her. The guilt was already setting in and she wasn't even there yet. I kept weeping and couldn't control the tears as they rolled down my cheeks, I was an emotional wreck. We got in the car with my mum without informing her of what was happening otherwise she would have never agreed, and we just hoped she was accepting of the circumstances once she was there.

A Stepping Stone to Her New Found Home

On the way to the home, I borrowed my sister's sunglasses to hide my eyes. I was really struggling to hold myself together in the car and knew that leaving my mum at this home was going to be heart-breaking. I didn't want her to see me getting upset and didn't really want anybody else seeing me crying if I could help it. We pulled up at some large metal automatic gates that opened as my car got close to them. As we drove towards the home I thought it looked pleasant, it was like an old manor house with a rustic edge. I was told to ring a number I was given to inform them when we had arrived so they could meet us outside. I rang the number and just waited in the car for them to show as there was more than one building so I wasn't quite sure what direction we needed to head towards. A few minutes later two members of staff came out of a side entrance of one of the buildings so we got everything out of the car and walked over to them. They introduced themselves and then took us through the side entrance that led to the place my mum would be staying.

As we walked in, we were led to what was the dining area, it felt very much like a school canteen the way it was set up. Everywhere was neutral in colour and quite boring looking. The floors were all hard floors and it gave me the same impression as the hospital. It made me feel sick that I had to leave my mum here and I was quite shocked that this home came highly recommended. It was OK but I thought it was going to be so much better, I was disappointed. All I kept thinking was about how lovely and homely Alderwood was and I couldn't understand why no other home fulfilled this. As we sat in the dining area I kept my shades on as tears slowly fell from my eyes. The staff that spoke to my sister were lovely, really friendly and made me feel a bit more at ease. They told us they would show us to my mum's room so we headed further up the corridor. On the way I saw a few other residents, there was one man walking up and down with a carer by his side. He had a blue soft helmet on his head and as he walked up and down he was leaning to the side so the carer was supporting him. As we walked past another man's room he was shouting out random words really loud, I was informed that was normal and he did it through the night too. There were a couple of older lady residents walking round together chatting and laughing which was a delight to see. The corridors appeared a bit bigger than the hospitals which meant more room for my mum to walk around, and I also saw a door right near her bedroom that opened onto an outside seating area. This made me slightly happier because at least she wasn't stuck indoors if she didn't want to be. As we walked into her room I was pleasantly surprised by the size of it, it was spacious and with an en-suite. There was a wardrobe, chest of draws, table and a bed. The bed was in the middle of the room with the headboard against the wall so my sister and I decided to move it so that the side of the bed was against the wall. This was to try and prevent my mum from falling out like she did in the past. I placed a few of the pictures I had packed from my parent's house on top of her new chest of drawers. I knew her stay was temporary but I wanted her to feel at home and to know we cared. I made a list of all of her belongings, put them all away and then gave the list to the senior carer. He was lovely, very friendly and able to answer any questions I had. He informed me that my mum would be receiving 1 to 1 care which meant she would have a career with her at all times. At the time I felt this was a good thing because I thought she would get more care, help and attention regarding her needs. I wasn't quite sure why the 1 to 1 was in place but looking back I think it was probably because my mum had been sectioned twice and maybe there were unsure of how she was going to react.

Before we left, I asked the staff where the large garden area was, and they pointed to a door that was a few metres from my mum's room. My sister and I went to have a quick look and it did not feel like the same garden that I had seen pictures of. There was a small flat area of grass and the rest was slightly uphill with an uneven and rocky path all the way up. There was absolutely no way my mum would have been able to go outside on her own to take a walk around without falling over. She wasn't the most co-ordinated on a flat even path so this was just a trip hazard in my eyes. It was a shame because the scenery was lovely but it just wasn't practical. I was informed that there was an alarm that was triggered if anybody did go outside, so that the staff knew a resident was in the garden.

After having a look around and feeling slightly apprehensive about my mum staying in this home, it was time to say goodbye. I told her that we were going and she got upset asking why she had to stay there. I tried to explain that she wanted to be able to do her own thing and said she didn't want to be at home with my dad, so we had no other option. She started getting more upset and it was very clear she didn't want to be left but I knew I had no choice. I was distraught that I couldn't take my mum back to her home and that I had to abandon her once again. I was breaking inside and felt like I had let her down. I couldn't bear to see her upset, so I said my goodbyes, gave her a hug and walked off leaving my sister with her. I made my way out of the home and back to the car. I was utterly inconsolable and never thought I would find that day as tough as I did. A few minutes later my sister came out and we made our way home acknowledging the change that had just occurred.

The following day my sister and I went back to see my mum and see how things were going. As we arrived in the building we could see her just pacing up and down the corridor quite distressed, but I was expecting that with the change of environment. She was happy to see us and when I suggested going for a hot chocolate and she was overjoyed. We got her in the car, and took her 10 minutes up the road to Costa. I got her a piece of cake and a hot chocolate and I think we all forgot for a few minutes what was happening because we were away from the situation and chatting like nothing had happened. We then went round a shop and got my mum some bottles of water and chocolate to have in her room so that she could help herself to a drink and a treat when she wanted one. When we got back to the home I was asked by a member of staff to collect my mum's medications and bring them with me when I next visited because she was running low. I agreed and said I would bring them up the following day. As I was talking to the carer my mum was getting really frustrated with the guy standing next to her. He was her 1 to 1 carer and she was far from impressed. She kept muttering, 'I don't know why he keeps following me.' She would then just walk off and the carer followed a few steps behind her, even I felt it was a bit excessive. It was that time of the visit where I had to say goodbye again. I gave her a hug and she started crying once more, I tried to reassure her I would be back and that she was OK but she was so distressed. I couldn't hack it and walked off again leaving my sister with her. I felt like my heart was being ripped out and trodden on every time I had to leave her crying and upset and I just hoped that it would get easier. The image of leaving her sobbing was lingering in my memory for far too long and I couldn't switch off when I got home.

My dad was still in Manchester and my sister was away for a whole week so it was down to me to look after my mum, making sure she was being cared for, find a new home and remind her she was not forgotten. I was not going to put her into a home 40 minutes away and then just leave her there without going to see her. I was upset that I was the only family member there to look after her but I understood why my dad couldn't face the situation at that moment in time. Every single day I went to see her without fail, I also told work I wouldn't be in because I was too busy looking for a care home for my mum and wasn't sure what day I would have to move her to a different home. I didn't want to keep messing them about by going back and then needing another day off, and to be honest my mind was well and truly elsewhere at the time. At the weekends I went to see my mum with Shaun and the kids so that they were not missing out on my time with them and to keep things as normal as possible for my mum. It was also important to me for my children to see the decline in nanny so that they didn't have a shock when they did eventually see her. Everything my mum does when the kids are around her is normal to them because they see nanny so often and they are used to seeing me helping her. We had some really fantastic days with my mum whilst she was in the home and we made the most of what there was to do in the area whilst we were there.

One lovely hot Saturday we went to the supermarket on the way to the home and got loads of food so that we could have a picnic in the garden. When we got there we laid out a blanket and placed all the food onto it. We got some chairs and I put music on my phone. It was such a lovely afternoon and my mum was finally smiling and laughing again. The kids enjoyed it and so did she and it's one of those memories I will cherish. On the Sunday we decided to go to a place that had a kids playcentre inside and it was only 10 minutes up the road. I sat with my mum at a table drinking hot chocolate whilst Shaun and the kids ran around playing. We all had lunch and then I took her over to a shop outside and got her some egg custards and chocolate. It was another lovely day and I felt so happy that as a family we shared it with my mum. I'm not saying it was easy and I'm not saying it was perfect because it wasn't but I did it for her. She tried to get up and walk off on occasions, she dropped her food on the floor, and I had to care for her whilst she was with me which was hard work. However seeing my mum smile, knowing I was breaking her tedious day up for her, knowing she was getting to see some familiar faces, and giving her all the things she loved made me feel happy. Alzheimer's was trying to destroy her life, it was breaking her marriage, it had taken her home and taken her independence. Well I was going to do my utmost to give her the best and the happiest life she could live with this sickening disease.

After a couple of days and once the weekend was over I was informed that they would be taking the 1 to 1 off my mum as they felt it was making her more anxious and uneasy having somebody follow her around and they didn't think she needed it. This was such good news and after a few days she appeared less tense and much happier. I spent the next week taking my mum out with Charlotte to a little garden centre up the road for a hot chocolate and a slice of cake, or to the Costa for her usual. I drove her to MacDonald's for lunch one day and even sat with her when she had lunch in the home on another. The week was passing by really quickly. One day when I showed up to take her out she was walking like she had pulled her back out, leaning over to one side. I was told by the carers that the doctor would be there shortly to take a look and see how she could help.

146

When the doctor showed up she assessed my mum and had a look at her back. The carer then informed the doctor that my mum was struggling to go for a wee. This was news to me, but I listened to what the carer had to say. They said that when she sat on the toilet she was straining but couldn't wee and the doctor looked concerned because it was probably connected to her back hurting. I was so glad I was there for the doctor visiting my mum and I disagreed with what the carer said. I explained that she generally went for a wee in her pad and that if she was told to go for a wee she because she probably couldn't remember and didn't realise she had already done it in her pad. It was quite normal for her to have a sore back and for as long as I could remember she had suffered from time to time with it. This to me was just another example of being able to provide better care for her because I had an understanding. I had learnt so much about her and watched her change with the Alzheimer's every single day, and this enabled me to make decisions with her best interests at heart. The doctor was happy with what I had to say and just prescribed paracetamol for my mum. I was told that it wouldn't be available until the following day, however, I wasn't letting my mum go through any pain for another whole day. I decided to get in my car and drive to the local newsagent to get her some pain relief. I drove back to the home and gave my mum two tablets. I informed the carers and they were more than happy and I gave them the box of paracetamol so that they could give her some more later on that day. Unfortunately that wasn't the only problem I encountered whilst visiting her.

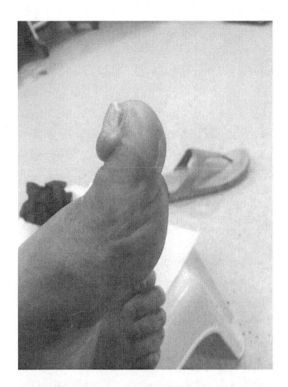

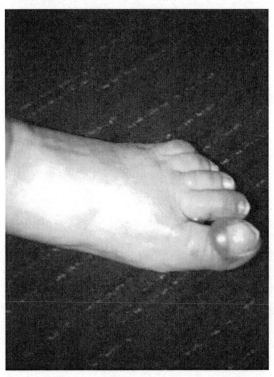

I decided I was going to take my mum out for lunch, so I drove to the home and picked her up. Before we left the carer informed me that her feet were a bit sore and they would get the doctor to look at them when they were next in. She had shoes on and was walking so I didn't think her feet could be that bad, how wrong was I? When we got to the restaurant I sat my mum down with charlotte at a table as I ordered the food. Whilst we were waiting I could see she was in some sort of discomfort so I asked her if she was OK. She told me that her feet were hurting so I thought I had better check them and see what the carer was on about. I removed her shoes and her socks and was in absolute utter disbelief in what I was seeing. I was so distraught that I stood up from the table and took a few steps away to gather my thoughts before I continued to talk to her. Her toes had the biggest blisters on them that I had ever seen, and I was angry that they had been left like that. I was told that the doctor would look at them when they were next in but that just wasn't good enough. My mum was suffering, I strongly believed she needed antibiotics, and there was absolutely no way she was suffering any longer than she had to. I took a picture of her feet and emailed it to the social worker and she rang me. I asked her what I should do because I couldn't leave her in pain. I made the suggestion that I booked my mum into the doctors she was still registered too and she agreed. The food came out but my appetite was gone, my mum on the other hand was hungry so I let her eat her meal and Charlotte joined her by stuffing her face with whatever she could get her hands on. Whilst they were eating I rang the doctors to get an appointment. When I got through they tried to tell me I couldn't have an appointment because they were all gone, but I explained the situation and told them she needed to be seen that day. They eventually agreed for a nurse to take a look at my mum's feet at 3.30p.m. so we had a few hours to wait. I rang the home and informed them that I had a doctor's appointment for my mum and that she wouldn't be back until later on that day. When we had finished lunch we got in the car and I drove to my house where I hoped she would sit and wait until it was time to leave. She sat down on the sofa, I made her a cup of tea, put loose woman on the tv and put her feet up onto a foot rest. She did try to get up and wanted to leave a few times but she did listen when I politely asked her to sit down and wait for the appointment.

Time soon passed and we were sat waiting at the doctors surgery for my mum to be seen. We were not waiting long before we were called in. As soon as the nurse saw her she couldn't believe how bad and painful her toes looked. She said she was going to prescribe some antibiotics and that she would need to get someone else to pop the blisters and dress them. We were told the prescription would be brought downstairs to us whilst we were in with the other nurse. The blisters were popped and dressed lightly and then we headed to the main reception to wait for the prescription. I thought things were going relatively well and then my mum started getting agitated. We were waiting for about 20 minutes for the prescription to be sent down to the main desk, and she was walking off, talking to herself and becoming annoyed. I had to keep asking her to stop walking off and to wait and everybody was staring at us both. I think this is where people's perceptions need to change because they see someone my mum's age and they just assume she is mentally unwell, they never expect it to be Alzheimer's. On occasion I have told people she has Alzheimer's when she has got irritated and started muttering to herself and they are always so shocked. I was getting to the point where I wanted to just cry and walk off in the doctors because my stress levels were becoming unbearable. I was sick of waiting around, tired or being stared at, and scared of losing my mum if I turned my head for 5 seconds. I also had charlotte with me so I had my hands full and I was struggling to cope. Finally the prescription was brought to us and I then had to get into another queue at the pharmacy. My mum was walking around the pharmacy and kept trying to walk out of the other exit. I was trying to keep my eyes on her, watch charlotte, keep my place in the queue and keep calm whilst all eyes were on me. I remember emailing the social worker explaining how upset I was and how angry I felt with the situation I was in. I felt I should have been given priority with my mum, I should not have had to endure such a long wait and neither should she. If only they understood what doctors and hospitals caused for her and how they increased her anxiety which in turn made it so much harder for me. When I left the doctors surgery I was at breaking point, I just wanted to drop her back and go home to relax, it had been a long day.

My mum had really started settling into the home and I felt more at ease with the choice I made and the routine I had formed. She was starting to get a rapport with a couple of the carers and one in particular she grew fond of. I would walk into the dining room to find my mum almost crying with laughter because this particular lady was telling her jokes or messing about. It was really nice to see and made the situation easier for me knowing she was being made to laugh the way she was by my dad when she was at home. Although she was settling in nicely I knew it wasn't permanent and I needed to find somewhere permanently for her. I got sent another list of homes from the social worker and took a look around about 4. My sister came in the car with me whilst I went into the homes and she stayed in the car with the children. One home was absolutely awful and there was no chance my mum was going into that one. As soon as I walked through the front doors I was hit with the disgusting smell of cabbage and urine. It took 2 minutes to show me round because it was so tiny and as I walked down the small corridor and looked into the rooms everybody looked like they were at the end of life. There was nobody walking around, no sounds, it was bleak and sad. I wanted to be polite by looking around but I instantly knew there wasn't a chance on this planet my mum would be residing there. I thanked the receptionist for her time and got back to the car. It was a definite no for me and no words could fully describe how bad it was.

The others were OK but compared to Alderwood they were mediocre. Just regular old care homes with not much to do and I just couldn't imagine my mum living in them. Alderwood was in another league and now that I had viewed it, I was finding it really hard to accept her going into anywhere else. I decided to go back to the care home I visited the first time and told my sister to come in this time so that I could get someone else's perception. I knew that although it wasn't a patch on Alderwood, it was better than anywhere else I had visited so far. My sister and I got shown around and she was happy enough with what she had seen. She thought it was nice, modern and more open than the home she was currently in so we filled in the paperwork and they said they would do an assessment on my mum. We knew time was of the essence and we were running out of options, we didn't want the decision to be taken out of our hands. I felt relieved that we had finally come to a decision and that compared to the other homes that we had the choice of, this one was better for my mum. I was still really gutted about Alderwood but knew I needed to move forward and be happy that she was going somewhere nice. I felt a sense of relief and was coming to terms with the decisions I had made. However everything was about to be thrown up into the air again when after a few days the care home I wanted for her did the assessment and then said no. When I rang to find out why it turned out they didn't have any beds. I was gobsmacked that they had wasted my time, upset that my plans had come crashing down once again and angry that my poor mum was now back to square one. I was absolutely gutted.

I phoned the social worker and told her that I had visited numerous care homes and I couldn't see my mum in any of them. She told me not to worry and she gave me the name of another care home to visit. I was starting to lose faith and began feeling panicked that this decision was being put on me and I didn't want to rush it. So one morning my sister and I went to this other care home. It was a small little building with numerous buildings surrounding it. I was greeted by a kind friendly lady who spoke in depth to me about my mum and her needs. As we walked towards the bedrooms and main seating area I just couldn't put my finger on why I was not feeling positive about the place. It was clean and bright but it was also quite small and all the residents were again very old and just sitting in chairs around the tv. They were throwing a small ball to each other which I think was part of one of the activities for that day. I just knew my mum would be so bored here and again it lacked a homely feel. I also knew my options were limited so I started to think, was I being too critical? Did I need to just accept that my mum would be in one of these homes? On the other hand I was thinking she was only 55, she needed the best, something with a bit of life and soul. This would be the place she would be calling her home for the remainder of her life and I couldn't accept second best, she deserved more than that. I walked out of the building and told my sister how I felt, she told me that if I didn't feel 100% then I shouldn't settle and not to rush. I then had more determination than ever before that my mum was getting the best, so I took a leap of faith and decided to swing by Alderwood one last time.

As we pulled up in the car park I was wasn't expecting much but I had to try. I went to the reception desk and explained that I needed a space for my mum and I was desperate. She told me to take a seat and wait to speak with the manager Nikki. My heart was pounding and I wanted this home even more now that I was sat here. There were residents walking towards the brasserie, carers smiling and laughing with them, and there was still a lovely scent surrounding me. I wanted this home so bad, I felt like I was almost teasing myself coming back in again. A few minutes later I was greeted by Nikki who was friendly and very approachable. We spoke for a short while about my mum and my situation, and Nikki explained that there weren't any beds available just yet. I tried to remain strong and brave but then my emotion became too much and I got tearful. I wanted this home for her more now than when I first saw it. I explained to Nikki that she was in a temporary care home 40 minutes away and I was struggling to go and see her every day. I told her how my mum needed to find a home closer to us so that we could try and continue a normal life as much as possible, but I wasn't prepared to put her in any other homes I had viewed. I also spoke about how we were let down by one home that did the assessment and then said they had no beds, which had delayed the process for us. I expressed how much she meant to me with tears rolling from my eyes, and how I felt she had suffered enough without having to be stuck in a home that I knew wasn't good enough. I described how Alzheimer's had taken so much of my mum away, but she still had use of her legs and needed the space and activities to keep her occupied. She had always been a lady of good taste and I knew if she could make the decision herself she would have loved Alderwood because it had class. I told Nikki I would do anything for my mum and I owed it to her to get her a place in Alderwood and if I couldn't, I didn't know what I was going to do. I was under immense pressure to make a decision because where she was currently was only temporary. I poured my heart out about how most of the other homes had lovely reception areas and appeared homely but this wasn't continued throughout the rest of the home. Alderwood was different and every single inch of the home was filled with thought and love. Nikki listened with care, compassion and understanding and I believe she saw I was near breaking point that day. She went into her office, made a phone call and came back. She gave me a reassuring smile and told me the happiest news I had heard in a long time, 'Your mum has a room here, if I can get confirmation from the social worker and an email with all the paperwork.' I was absolutely over the moon and Nikki will never realise what she did for me and my family that day. I was so happy, it was the first time in ages I had a real reason to smile. I finally felt like my mum was having a bit of good luck for a change. I felt like a weight had been lifted off my shoulders and I knew my dad would be so relieved. I couldn't actually quite believe that I made the decision to pop into Alderwood that day and it paid off. It was explained that she would need to have an assessment done first but I was confident this would run smoothly, I had told Nikki everything about my mum that she would need to know. I was so overjoyed it made me even more tearful, so I took Nikki's number and email before thanking her and leaving. I stepped outside and let out a huge cry of relief and happiness. When I got back into the car I think my sister must have thought something had gone very wrong, I was so upset, but I explained they were tears of happiness and that my mum had got a place in Alderwood. We were both so pleased and I got straight on the phone to the social worker to let her know the good news and put the wheels in motion.

The next day Nikki informed me that she had received the relevant paperwork and she would be assessing my mum in a couple of days' time. I was given a time and date so that I could also be present. I couldn't believe that everything was falling into place and I started to feel like I could breathe again. I was hoping that if all went well she would be able to move into Alderwood quite quickly. Before then we had a few days before the assessment and my dad was back from Manchester so we went to see my mum in the home. We took her to Costa one day, and a garden centre on another. She seemed more relaxed with my dad and wasn't being cold and frosty towards him like she was. Seeing them holding hands walking into the garden centre was so heart-warming and felt like old times. My dad didn't go into the actual home more than once because he felt it reminded him of a hospital and he couldn't face it. It upset him when he had to leave and he didn't like seeing my mum walking back and forth up the corridor. So I would always run in and get her whilst my dad sat in the car.

Then came the morning of the assessment, I was excited but apprehensive at the same time. My sister and I decided we would both be there for the assessment and we had a few of the kids with us too. Nikki arrived and made me feel very much at ease, she looked relaxed and friendly. She sat with my mum for a few minutes before she got up and started walking up and down because she, 'had work to do.' In the few minutes she spoke to her, Nikki got a laugh and a smile from her and also had a conversation about the "blokes" that my mum knew. Although she wasn't making much sense, Nikki just went with the flow and made it feel like we were all living in the same reality for those few minutes. That was all Nikki needed to see and she had made her mind up, she informed me that my mum would be able to move into Alderwood. She said it would probably be at the beginning of the following week which was a few days away. I was so relieved and happy because this was the confirmation we needed, and then the countdown begun.

The last few days flew by and it was eventually the day for my mum to move into Alderwood. I was so nervous about how she would take to being moved somewhere new but also so excited for her to be in a home she deserved. I drove to a shop on the way to get my mum some lunch, got a bottle of champagne for Nikki to say thank you and some sweet treats and cakes for the staff at the home my mum was currently in. I was grateful to the staff for looking after her for the last few weeks and for being so warm and welcoming. When I walked into the home the staff had told my mum she was going to a new home but I don't think she had processed the information, she was just accepting what they were telling her rather than understanding it. I went to her room and the staff helped me pack up her belongings and get her ready to leave. I gave them their cakes and treats and thanked them for looking after her. They told me that they would miss her, that she had been a pleasure to look after and that the other home was lucky to have her. That was really nice to hear because the Alzheimer's was stripping my mum's personality away piece by piece but the kind, funny, lovely lady was still there somewhere. We said our goodbyes before a couple of the staff gave me a hand with everything to the car. I informed the social worker that I was on my way to Alderwood as she supportively offered to meet me at the home, she knew I was nervous about my mum's reaction. We then began the drive to the fresh start that awaited her.

She Deserved the Best, We Hoped For Good, She Got 'Outstanding'

It was now the beginning of June 2019 and we finally had something to smile about, my mum was finally moving into a home that would give her the space, care and understanding that she needed. It had been a long 18 months and I felt as a family we were due some good luck, and we were finally getting some. As we walked through the doors of Alderwood, the social worker was waiting for us and so was Nikki. My mum appeared to be taking the move quite well. She wasn't getting upset or questioning what was happening. We were showed to my mum's bedroom and I sat her in a chair. The room had a single bed, a bedside table, a wardrobe and some comfy chairs to sit on. As I walked further into the room I spotted the sweetest kindest gesture, the home had got my mum fresh flowers for her room, some chocolates, ginger biscuits, and a welcome card. It was so lovely to see and another example of how wonderful this home was, so much effort was put into every single detail. The deputy manager came in and said hello and handed me some forms to fill in. She asked if we needed anything and said to make a list of everything my mum had brought with her. I began labelling everything and writing everything down so that I could put it all away and start settling my mum in. I asked if I could decorate the room just to double check and I was informed that I could do what I wanted with the room. I had so many ideas already and her room was going to be made to look just like it would if she was at home. My mum happily sat in a chair whilst I sorted out her belongings and it made it slightly easier for me that my she wasn't questioning the situation because I didn't want to have to explain what was happening in case it upset her. I knew it was an extremely sad time with her moving out of the family home, but she was, in my opinion, in the best home in Colchester without a doubt. The social worker left us to it, and I rang my dad to let him know that my mum was in the home and he should come down and see it. He came to see the home and I could see he was heartbroken, however I could also see that he was delighted with the home. He told me it was lovely and he couldn't wish for any better and that was without him viewing some of the homes I had to endure. My dad sat on the bed with my mum and held her tight, he knew he would be spending many more hours in this room with her and it was now her new home for the foreseeable.

As my dad and I left Alderwood that first day it was hard, really hard. I couldn't even imagine how I would have felt if she wasn't in there and she ended up in one of the others. I did feel like I had abandoned my mum even though I knew she was in the best place, a lovely place. I felt like the Alzheimer's had won and we had broken, we weren't strong enough. What I realise now is that my mum is actually happier, she has more space, she still does what she used to do on a daily basis and she is cared for amazingly, and this is far more than what she was getting at home. I made a promise to myself that I would not let her feel alone or left behind and I would visit her as much as I possibly could. For the first few months this was twice a day and it helped with my guilt and it made me feel involved in my mum's care because I was seeing it first-hand every day. However, I soon realised I was letting it consume my whole life and now generally I visit only once a day. My dad and I decided my mum's room was going to be completely redecorated and he told me to get whatever was needed to make her room, her home. I told my dad that Shaun and I would decorate the room to make it modern, classy and homely. My dad also suggested we ordered a double bed as my mum wasn't used to sleeping in a single bed and had a tendency to roll around in the night a lot. We ordered that straight away and had it delivered directly to the home. Once we had been to several shops and had everything we needed, Shaun and I spent one whole evening completely changing her room. We painted the back wall in a chic rose gold and grey on a wall next to it. We had some matching accessories, picture frames for the walls, a new comfy grey chair, a matching glitzy grey footstall, some silver velvet curtains and a grey duvet set for her new double bed. Shaun put the bed together whilst I continued painting, whilst we both had to try and watch Charlotte as she loved touching the wet paint tray and then touching walls we didn't want painting. It was hard work and we got most of what we needed to get done that evening, but Shaun went back on the weekend to finish those last few bits.

Once the room was completed, it really did start feeling like my mum's home. My dad and I went in some evenings and sat with her and ordered a takeaway pizza and put the tv on like we would have when she was at home with him, we tried keeping things as normal as possible. We tried to take her out to Costa in the mornings as much as possible and me and my sister would sometimes take her to McDonald's or somewhere for lunch so that she was still getting out whilst she was able to. The staff initially informed us that my mum wasn't really eating a lot. She would not sit still for more than a few minutes and they would chase her up and down the corridors with food and drink on the go. This was the situation for a few weeks whilst she was settling in. She was definitely anxious and confused about the move initially and it was very hard to say goodbye at the end of a visit. She would say, 'why where are we going,' or 'come on then let's go.' It would distress me so much because I had to try and explain that I was leaving and she wasn't. I would try and explain that I would be back the following day and she would just look disappointedly at me and then accept what I was saying. The look of upset and confusion was making it so difficult that I started waiting for her to turn her back and then just getting into

159

the lift quickly before she saw. That was so that I didn't have to say the heart-breaking goodbye and didn't need to see the pain on her face that I was leaving her. I was spending so much time with my mum, and I was still finding it hard to adjust initially, that was when I decided to quit work. I liked my job at royal mail but if my mum's illness taught me anything, it was that life was too short. I wanted to be there for her morning, noon and night if it was needed of me and work was restricting me. I thought about my dad at home on his own and knew he wouldn't cook for himself so it was down to me to continue to look after him. If I was at work I was rushing meal times and felt under pressure to get things done, so after thinking about it for weeks and weeks and with the support of Shaun and my dad, I decided to leave work. I felt a sense of relief and like a weight had been lifted so I used my spare evenings go and see my mum. Times when I know I made the right decision include receiving a phone call in the evening to say my mum had fallen and she was in a worked up and anxious state. I jumped in the car to see her and to reassure her everything would be OK. I helped to calm and relax her and eventually she would forget all about what just happened. I had the freedom to be there for my mum regardless of the time or day because I didn't have work to answer to.

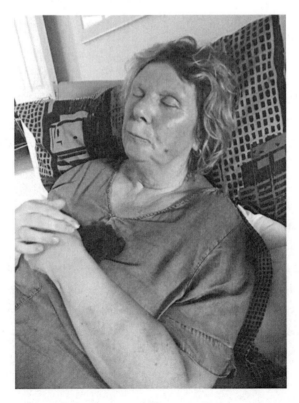

It wasn't long before she had her first obvious decline in Alderwood. I received a call from the home telling me she had fallen over and was now leaning as she was walking. They said that she was really distressed and getting really worked up. It was only 20 minutes until Shaun got home so I said I would be straight down as soon as he was home. I was really hoping she was OK when I got there because as I'm sure you have now established I cannot cope with seeing my mum in any pain or distress. When I got there she was walking up the corridor, she was leaning so far backwards and to the side she could have given the limbo world record holder a run for their money. As she turned round to see me she burst into tears and hugged me tightly. She started breathing heavily and getting herself into a panic. I kept hold of her and told her it was OK, whilst I was wandering in my own head, 'was my mum OK?' I cried a few tears of my own because I just wanted to take her anxiety away and I didn't know how I could help her. Seeing her in such a distressed and awful state was so upsetting because I just wasn't expecting her to look as bad as she did. I walked her back to her room and sat her in a chair, whilst the staff went and got some cold flannels to put on her face. She was so hot and had worked herself up so much I just needed to calm her and cool her down a bit. After just a few minutes of me arriving she calmed down and started to return to a slightly more normal colour. I gave her a drink and she then stood up and began wandering the corridors again. Her back appeared to already be better than it was and she was more upright than before. I stayed for a short while and told the staff to ring me if there were any problems.

The following day my sister and I went to take my mum to Costa. Her back seemed better than the previous day but she seemed to be a million miles away. She wasn't looking where she was going, she was unable to co-ordinate taking items out of my hand, she was nearly falling over and was very slow. Something didn't seem right, but I had learned to accept that my mum had good and bad days and some days were a lot worse than others. After quite a few attempts I got her into the car and took her to Costa up the road. We had breakfast and she was missing her mouth with her drink, nearly fell off her chair and wasn't engaging in any conversations. It was like she was on a completely different planet altogether, she even kept falling asleep and then waking up again. I started thinking that maybe there was more to what was going on and I was glad the doctor was going to take a look at her later on that day about her back. I decided to take her back to her home so that we didn't miss her time with the doctor. As I stood my mum up from her chair it felt like she had declined further. She was unable to stand up straight and was unaware she was pulling backwards. My sister had walked out of the Costa with Charlotte and was waiting outside. The Costa was so busy and I was trying to direct my mum out of the door whilst keeping her from falling over. As I got half way towards the door she started leaning back further and I couldn't hold her body weight. I was trying to tell her to stand up but she wasn't acknowledging any instructions given to her and pulling further towards the ground. I was using all my strength to bring her back up straight but I couldn't, I was stuck. I had her two hands and just kept hold of her so that she didn't fall but I couldn't move. I was so upset because nobody in the shop acknowledged my struggle, people were standing nearby and just carrying on with their days. I felt so lost, trapped and upset that I just stood there and broke down. I was pleading with my mum through tears and desperation to stand up straight but she may as well have been asleep. Eventually a lady on a table at the back of the shop came over to me and asked if I was OK, I wept and muttered that I wasn't and that my mum had Alzheimer's. She got her from behind and supported some of her weight and then was trying to get her into a chair that was behind her. The more we tried to help the more she was pulling towards the ground. A few seconds later, my sister came back into the shop and asked what was going on, she told everyone, including the lady helping to move away and give her some space and then took control of the situation. I know my sister reacts in a rude way sometimes and when things are stressful she loses her manners, she would agree herself. What she didn't realise, was that without that lady's help I don't know what I would have done. My mum could have fell, I could have fell and I would have most definitely been more of an emotional wreck than I already was. That lady renewed my faith in humanity that day. Proof that people can help and support others when times are tough without judgement. I thanked the lady and she went back to her seat but I would love to thank her again, so thank you! My sister and I started heading towards the door and it took about 5 minutes to get her to step her feet over the threshold. Its sounds such a simple thing to do but my mum seemed to have lost her normal body functions like walking and stepping. It took my sister and another lady to get her feet through the door and onto the pavement outside. It then took a further 5 minutes to get my mum down the curb and over to the car which was 10 metres away, and 5 minutes to get her in the car. All with the help of another lady who again was great and very supportive. It took several attempts to get her into the car, in the end I had to pull from the driver's side and my sister was pushing from my mum's side. We got in the car and breathed a sigh of relief, however we needed answers about why my she had declined so badly.

I informed the staff about the traumatic trip out and they explained that they would get a urine sample, the doctor would take a look at my mum, and they would phone me later to let me know the results. A few hours later I received a call to tell me that she had a urine infection, and that she had been prescribed antibiotics. I was so relieved because every time I saw her decline I always hoped there was a cause for the decline rather than it just being part of the Alzheimer's. At least then I knew she could get better and it wasn't a permanent decline. I knew I wouldn't be able to take her out for a while whilst she had the infection because I could not face another trip out like the last one. I continued to visit and after a few weeks, and an increase in the strength of antibiotics she was back to where she was before the infection.

Although I love taking my mum out because I feel it is good for her to get out whilst she is still able to, Alderwood puts on so many activities and events that when the day comes and my mum isn't able, she will still have a very fulfilled life. Whilst she has been in there I have seen numerous agency singers who have been amazing. Some weekends I go and spend quality time with my mum whilst also getting to enjoy someone singing some great classic tracks. I have seen some cute fluffy animals be brought in for the residents to hold and stroke, I took my kids along and they loved it too. I have never felt like my children are not welcome and I have finally been able to spend time with my mum and my family together. I have had picnics in the beautiful garden with her Shaun and the kids, I've attended garden parties where toys were laid out for the kids and a paddling pool was set up. My mum and the other residents love seeing the children, especially Charlotte. They love a baby and she gets all the attention whenever she is with me. Alderwood put on fun for the whole family and they don't do anything by halves. The summer fayre was absolutely amazing, with burgers, hot dogs, ice cream, sweets for the children, a gin stand, a puppet show, dancers and so much more. So much effort is put into every event and they are always absolutely amazing. On bonfire night the fireworks were better than any display I have been to for a long time, a singer entertained us, and we got to have jacket potatoes and hot dogs. They didn't forget about the children either providing them with a huge bucket filled with sparklers and a table laid out with sweets. The Christmas fayre had a magician for the children, cakes and they even got Santa to visit. I could go on and on about the all the activities and the thought and effort that goes into each and every activity for the residents but I would get very jealous. Whilst the residents are going bowling, to the cinema or to the pub I am sat at home only wishing my life was as half as exciting as theirs.

For my mum's birthday in September, Nikki got her amazing team to organise a small party. It really was exceptional and filled with so much thought and effort. They organised a singer to come in and sing some more youthful songs from my mum's era, they put on food, drink and they brought out a birthday cake. They also gave her some lovely gifts on her birthday which I really didn't expect. My aunty Sue and my cousin came down from Manchester so that they could spend time with my mum on her birthday. There wasn't many of us for the party just Shaun, our kids, my dad, Elaine, my aunty Sue and cousin, but the residents also joined us which was lovely and created the perfect atmosphere. It was such a special moment seeing my mum sat with those that cared and seeing her sat at the end of the table holding my dad's hand. I know I sounds very pessimistic but I couldn't help thinking I had to make the most of my mum's birthday because nobody knows how many more she will have. When the singer started singing I had a moment and got upset. I tried my best to conceal my tears but my mum noticed I was crying and asked if I was upset. I told her I was fine and she believed me. I then walked into the toilet so that I could get my emotions under control, I didn't know why I was so emotional but I needed to cry and get it out of my system. Seeing my mum happy and smiling, completely unaware of what her future held and listening to beautiful songs with my family was overwhelming for me. I was so happy to celebrate my mum's birthday with her but so sad at the same time. After a few minutes of trying to contain my emotions I then re-joined the party and enjoyed the moment with my family.

Since my mum has become ill I have spent so much time crying, I have cried when she has gone downhill but also when she is happy. Sometimes I watch her laughing and smiling and it brings me to tears. I don't know if it's because I know she is unaware of what her future holds. Her life is going to be cut short by this disease and she has no idea how much it has changed her already. When she is happy it's lovely but I know it's not the person my mum once was. Alderwood didn't only make my mum's birthday extra special they also made our first Christmas without my mum at home so much easier to manage. They explained that we could all come in as a family and they would cook a Christmas dinner for us so we thought that was brilliant. It saved us having to take my mum out to a restaurant and then her possibly getting anxious and then wanting to leave. Christmas day is also the one day of the year my brother spends with us and that is another stressful situation in itself. Shaun, the kids, my dad, my brother and I arrived to see my mum Christmas day. It was so wonderful the effort and time that had been put in, to make the day joyful. We had a table set up beautifully with crackers, including separate crackers for the children.

We had prosecco, wine and soft drinks and the food was perfect. They even got my mum a gift, wrapped it and placed it on her seat. We as a family couldn't wish for anything more. To be honest the whole home is magical at Christmas and the lights, decorations and displays are something to be desired. I have tried to include my mum in all events possible, bringing the kids in with their outfits on Halloween and getting her to write a valentines card for my dad on valentine's day. It's never easy and it's never as it should be but that is not going to stop me trying. She needs help with writing the valentines card out because she is unable to write anything anymore without assistance. I don't want her missing out on anything that she shouldn't have to and that she would have wanted to be involved in when she was well. I have taken her to the theatre a few times on the weekend and got her hair cut by my hairdressing friend Kerry, but none of it has been easy. In the theatre my mum was leaning so far over she was leaning onto the person next to her, she couldn't co-ordinate the steps, she was talking to herself and was dropping sweets all over the floor. When she last had her hair done she panicked about the foils near her face and she didn't want to put her head back to have her hair washed. I had to take her up to her room whilst she was apprehensive and upset to try and get the hair colour out of her hair. My mum was crying and not able to let me wet her hair because she was in such a state of panic. In the end I started losing patience and telling my mum to lean her head back, of course she couldn't do as I was asking because what may seem like a simple instruction is not simple to her. I ended up telling her to get out of the shower, she had only part of her hair wet and we were both drenched. A carer walked in and asked if we were OK to which I replied no and started crying. I was so angry with myself for not having the patience and so angry with the Alzheimer's for not allowing me to do nice things for my mum.

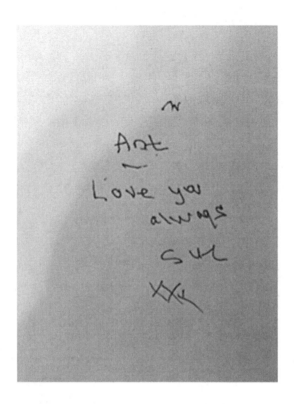

The longer my mum has been in Alderwood the more of an understanding I am getting for this awful disease. I see residents with dementia daily and see their struggles, the stages they are at, and how different they are but also how similar. One lady pushes chairs or trolleys up the corridors if she isn't holding onto someone, one lady goes round cleaning everything with her hands, and another seems so aware of everything I wouldn't have known she was a resident until she walked past her room several times because she had forgot where it was. There are so many different aspects to the disease that everyone is so different and I think their past still comes to light sometimes and this makes them all individual. When my mum first went into Alderwood I was introduced to a lady that I was told was only a few years older than my mum. She was so lovely but appeared much worse than my mum. She was very slow in her movements, lacked facial expressions and didn't hold much conversation. I took a shine to her right away because she seemed so lost and confused. Since then I have fed her, sat with her, put music on my phone for her and got Charlotte to be cute for her (that's getting harder as she's nearing 2 years old). I feel like seeing this lady is like looking into the future for my mum and it breaks my heart how much life and soul Alzheimer's has ripped from her. I have sat in a room with my mum and another resident whilst they have had a whole conversation and I didn't have a clue what they were talking about. The lady was saying about her home being built and how we all work hard, she was going to the home later and sometimes we didn't get what we needed. My mum was nodding her head and agreeing whilst talking about going to the shop and it wasn't far. Their conversations didn't match up and they were still happy having a conversation and it was beautiful to see. Another lady has asked me how old Charlotte was and if she was mine several times in about 5 minutes, whilst another cries when she sees her and says how much she reminds her of her children. I sometimes bring Charlotte to my mum's even when I have the option not to, just because she lights up the eyes of the residents every single time. It melts my heart time and time again and it almost makes me want to have another baby, and then I remember I have to actually take them home and decide against it.

I remember the first day I was walking up the corridors to find my mum and saw an empty room that was occupied a few days before. That was when my eyes really opened and I started thinking about my mum's future and what it had to bring. I asked a member of staff why the room was empty hoping that maybe there was another reason other than the inevitable, but it wasn't to be. They informed me the resident had passed away and I felt awful. It's not nice to hear about anybody passing away but knowing it was someone with dementia made me realise that this disease was ultimately a killer. Not only does it take pieces away of the person slowly turning them into a fraction of themselves but it eventually takes their life. It has passed through my head so many times about how long my mum has left but the reality of it is, that nobody knows. Something as minor as a fall can cause a huge decline and speed up the process, I have witnessed this with a few residents already. One lady was such a lovely, polite and chatty lady. I always noticed her because she carried a doll with her everywhere she went and sat on the same chair quite often. Then one day I came to see my mum and noticed that the lady was in bed and looking quite poorly and bruised. I really hoped she was OK and asked a member of staff who informed me she had fell over and hit her face. I have learned so much from the staff by asking questions because I feel it helps me understand and learn. They explained how sometimes when residents had a bad fall, it would set them back and sometimes would result in them no longer eating or drinking. This would then ultimately cause their bodies to start shutting down. A day later I passed the room of the lovely lady and saw an empty bed. I was informed that she had passed away. I was absolutely gutted for her because it seemed so unpredicted. It made me want to wrap my mum in bubble wrap or get her to wear a crash helmet so that she was protected from any serious injury or fall. Falls and bumps are so likely for people with dementia because it messes with co-ordination, slows down movements, and makes them have limited space awareness. A simple attempt at sitting down on a chair or stepping over a step can result in a fall. This lady wasn't the only one that had deteriorated and unfortunately passed away due to a fall, it scares me so much. When I now see a vacant room, I know why its empty and it fills me with sadness and I just hope it's a long time before my mum's room becomes available.

It's now been over 2 years since my mum's diagnosis and it has been the worse time of my life. Seeing my mum decline quickly has made me savour the time I do spend with her. She is happy in Alderwood and life has become easier but the pain for us has never eased. I can now drop my mum back after taking her out and say goodbye and she is happy with that. She doesn't try to leave with me or question anything. Alderwood has become her home and she even sometimes says, 'I'm back home now,' when I pull the car up outside. My dad and I decided it was best we didn't take her back to their home once she went into Alderwood because we felt this could upset and confuse her and we didn't want that. Sometimes on my visits to my mum I don't take her out. On some occasions I will just sit with her and spend time with her because I feel she is unable to go out. I have taken her out whilst being quite sleepy before and her coordination is so bad, she ended up walking into a raised border and fell over. She didn't hurt herself but that was because I softened the fall by grabbing her, but I started to learn that I can't take the risk when I can see she is not functioning the way she normally is.

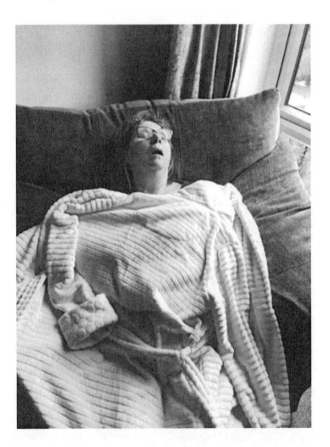

My mum has days now where she is very sleepy. The carers have had the doctor look at her several times because she has spent most of some days asleep.

She's had blood tests done and also had some medications reduced. The next medication the doctor was going to lower was my mum's anti-depressants but my dad and I disagreed. We advised that she had been on her depression pills for 15 years and they had never made her sleepy before, we didn't want her to become unhappy because we felt her mood was good. The bloods that were done we're fine and it does seem that this is just another part of the Alzheimer's taking hold. She has days where she walks the corridors up and down all day and I think it just takes its toll on her eventually. Some days she is very sleepy and falling asleep in whatever chair she is satin and other days she is very awake and doing lots of walking. I have been informed that my mum sleeps pretty well at night time. However she does go to bed a little later than she did at home and gets up a bit earlier so that is probably also making her tired. Tiredness is a very common thing to see, residents can be awake one minute and resting their eyes the next. If I wake my mum from a sleep she is unstable, not able to hold a conversation and more uncoordinated than what she normally is. My dad and I have been so grateful for the help and care from the exceptional staff at Alderwood. My dad struggles to see my mum sometimes because he is just trying to get his head around it all still, it breaks his heart seeing her walking up and down like a zombie. We were once told in a dementia meeting about mindfulness. It was explained that its best to try not to think about the future or the past and just concentrate on the here and now. I feel like it seems to others that I have got my head around my mum's illness and I'm OK, but I am not. I just try not to think about what lies ahead because when I do it upsets me and make me struggle with the day ahead. My mum's speech has become less coherent with time and a lot of conversations don't make sense, she uses a spoon to feed herself, she will trip or fall easily without support, she talks to herself a lot and she calls my dad, DAD. However she isn't eating liquidised food, she can still talk, walk and she does recognise the faces of her family still. She calls him dad because she hears me say dad all the time and that is now what she associates him with. I don't believe that she thinks he is her dad and she knows he is her husband. She has just forgot how much she loved him and always asks me, 'has he been good.' I always reassure her that he's always good and he would never ever hurt her or upset because he loves her so much. When my mum sees my children she knows who they are and when she sees me she usually gives me a hug and tells me she has been waiting for me or that she is so glad to see me and it makes her happy. If she doesn't show me that happiness or ignores me I will still go and spend some time each day with her but the pleasure she expresses when she sees me makes it so much easier. I do feel like my hard work and effort has paid off with her for now. I am fully expecting it not to last but for now I will take it and cherish it.

My mum is now drinking sugar in her tea and drinking coffee, both of which are not like her normally. She hasn't had sugar in her tea for about 30 years and doesn't drink coffee unless she is on a cruise and having one after her dinner. She will now eat most foods whereas up until a year or so ago, she absolutely hated anything with tomatoes or red sauce. She wouldn't touch lasagne or ketchup or anything in between, she wouldn't even wash pots that had been in contact with these foods. I now walk into the dining room and see her sat down with tomato-based dinners all the time, and I cannot believe it. Not only is my mum changing physically but she is changing as a person before my very eyes. Her likes and dislikes, her personality sometimes surprises me especially when she gets frustrated with somebody because she is normally so placid. Alderwood have kept her content and happy which is the most important thing and something I will always be grateful for. Something I believe everybody with Alzheimer's and their family should be able to be grateful for. I feel very strongly about everybody deserving the best care and home regardless of money. Whether somebody has a property to sell, or money in the bank, nobody deserves any less care than what Alderwood can offer. Alzheimer's is a devastating disease and no family needs the stress or worry about funding the very best care for their loved one. I feel the laws and rules need to change, all care homes should be homely and inviting with exceptional care and should be given free to all those who need it. My mum has been really lucky going into the best care home I have ever laid my eyes on but everybody should be as fortunate as she is regardless of wealth or circumstances.

The Obstacles of The Past, Present and Future

I can't describe my mum's time at Alderwood as perfect because a perfect situation would be for her to be at home with her family where she belongs. However, in the circumstances we have been handed, Alderwood has been so fantastic in every way. It's a care home to absolutely admire for its care, thought and understanding. They do their best by every situation they face and the residents are always their number one priority. This makes me feel rest assured that my mum is always receiving top quality care and I see this on a daily basis when I visit. Sometimes, when problems and situations from the past arise it makes me understand that although my mum doesn't express herself very well, she still has some of those same worries and concerns that she has had all her life. She hasn't forgotten about those. As previously mentioned, my mum has always been claustrophobic for the most part of her life. She never got on a plane, tried her hardest to avoid lifts, didn't like crowds, hated being locked in and even something like going into a public toilet, she would avoid locking the doors in case it got stuck and she got locked in. My mum has changed a lot since her diagnosis but she has never lost her hatred for small spaces. She started using the lift in the home so that I could take her out, but luckily it only takes a few seconds. I can see she doesn't like it, but the stairs are too much of a hazard now. She doesn't panic but she wants to get out as soon as the doors open, even if it means knocking somebody out the way to get out first. There's been a few occasions where she has concentrated so hard on getting out of the lift that she has knocked Charlotte over who she has forgotten is stood in-front of her. Her main aim is getting out of the lift and it becomes a tunnel vision for her, she is completely unaware of anything else around her until she is out of the lift.

My mum had always loved going to the hairdressers and nail bars and loved pampering herself on every occasion. My dad and I always wanted to keep her looking the way she always liked to with her highlights done and nails painted.

However, after the last time I got my friend Kerry to cut and colour my mum's hair I noticed she was a little bit more anxious than she normally was. I felt awful because I knew that I had made things so much worse for my mum getting her hair done. She was in tears that day and I made things ten times worse when I tried to shower her and the water was running in her face and my patience was wearing thin. Not only was my mum crying but I was too because the whole situation was painful and stressful. I couldn't cope with seeing my mum so unable to do anything, and I felt completely useless trying to get the bleach out of her hair when she didn't want to wash it out in the sink or in the shower. My mum was traumatised by the whole situation and I knew there and then I wasn't going to put her through that ever again. Kerry was fantastic with her but my mum was feeling trapped in the hairdressing chair for all the time required for a full head of highlights. I just wanted to make her feel special and to be treated the way she always was for all those years. I was beginning to understand that as long as my mum was happy, nothing else mattered. Grey hair, bed hair, no hair, it didn't matter as long as she was happy, healthy and loved. This was made worse by a fall in the corridor a day later and a fall out of bed the same night. The staff called me at home to inform me my mum had walked down the corridor and caught her foot on a piece of furniture and fell over. She wasn't hurt and they had checked her over but they did explain that she was really upset and panicked by the whole situation and it took a while for her to get up off the floor because she was so upset. I was confident in the knowledge that the staff would be doing all they could to calm my mum but I also knew my mum would appreciate me being there to assure her everything was OK. I told them I would come and see her and would be there in 15 minutes. I took some celebration chocolates out of the children's sweet tub and a sachet of hot chocolate powder I had in the back of the cupboard. If my smiley face couldn't cheer her up then I would go to plan B, chocolate.

I got to the home and walked around to find my mum. As I got into the dining area she was sat in a chair with a cup of tea, she was still crying. It broke my heart because again I felt like she shouldn't have to deal with a fall, or anything that sets her back because she has enough to deal with. I just want everything to be perfect for her because Alzheimer's is already taking so much away. When she saw my face she burst out crying and got up to hug me. I asked her if she had fallen over and she said yes and I asked if she was hurt and she said she hurt her leg. I told her I had hot chocolate in my bag and asked if she wanted to go and relax in her room with a nice drink, she agreed. She was really upset and red in the face, I just wanted to make sure she was OK and not in such an upset state before I left. As she got up and started walking, I was trying to observe her to see if she was showing signs of any injury but she appeared to be fine physically. As we were walking down the corridor to her room I saw one of the carers and they explained that my mum fell and was really upset. They believed it was more shock upset than actually hurting herself, and I agreed after seeing her walking like normal. They told me how she had got herself up after a few minutes using a chair to pull up on, and the staff supporting her. It's hard to imagine what was going through my mum's mind because she wouldn't have liked feeling trapped on the floor, she wouldn't have liked feeling disorientated falling to the floor, she wouldn't have liked people close around her helping her up, even though this was necessary. Her confidence would have taken a huge hit and I completely understood why she was so upset. Alzheimer's must make everything so much worse in her head and considering her phobia was bad enough before I could only imagine how she felt now. I took my mum into her room and got her to sit in her big comfy chair and I put her feet up on her foot stool. I opened up a few of the chocolates I took with me and rested them on the arm of the chair and then informed my mum I was going to make her a hot chocolate. By this point she had calmed down and seemed to have forgotten about her ordeal. I got back with her hot chocolate, placed it on the side table for her and turned on the tv. She never really watches the tv but it's always nice to have on in the background and to make things feel normal. After about half an hour she had eaten the chocolates, drank her hot chocolate and fell asleep. I was so relieved because I honestly could not have left her upset and I would have stayed there all night if I had to. I waited a few minutes longer to make sure she was definitely asleep and then I put on my coat and left.

The next morning when I went to see my mum the staff asked me if I knew about the fall and I said yes. They then started talking about how it might be worth getting a bed rail for the other side of her bed so that she can't fall out again. That was when we both realised we were not talking about the same fall and I was informed my mum had fell out of bed in the night and was extremely upset by it. I couldn't believe the bad luck my mum was having and hoped that she would be OK once I purchased a bed rail so that both sides of the bed were protected. My mum had a scrape down her arm and I was just relieved she didn't bang her head on anything and injure herself more seriously as she fell out. When

I saw my mum I noticed she seemed a bit more anxious and on edge that normal, she looked flustered and apprehensive. I told her my dad was out the front in the car and we were taking her out for a hot chocolate. I got her coat on and we got into the lift. This time was different to all the other times, my mum was panicked and started rapidly breathing. I assured her we were getting out again in just a few seconds and she was happy with that but it didn't make it any easier for her. When we got outside to the car, I opened up the car door and directed my mum into the front seat as I always did. Again something was different, she was stressed about crouching down into the car and was panicked at the idea of feeling trapped in the car. She eventually got in after a few words of encouragement and a couple of attempts. When we got to Costa we sat down to enjoy our drinks and cake but my mum was very unsettled. She kept getting hot and breathing quicker until eventually she got upset and said she wanted to leave. This was so unlike my mum and usually was the sign of a problem or underlying issue. We managed to settle her but it wasn't much longer until she said she wanted to leave again and stood up ready to leave. She was deeply distressed and it looked to me like she was feeling trapped in her own mind at this moment in time. I took my mum back to Alderwood and spoke to the staff about her unusual behaviour, they informed me they would get a urine sample from my mum to rule out an infection.

My dad and I went straight to a shop to purchase a bed rail so that my mum wouldn't have another fall out of bed again. We stopped by Alderwood on the way home and put the rail on the bed for her so that it was ready for the time she went to bed. My mum still seemed on edge, flustered and frustrated about something. She was walking up and down the corridor more frantically than normal and when she saw me she started crying and pulling at her jumper, like she was trying to get it away from her neck. I got her dressed into a lighter top so she didn't feel so weighed down by her jumper and could cool down. After getting her a drink, my dad and I left and hoped that she was either having a bad day or had an infection because otherwise it was feeling like my mum was on a decline and her problems with small spaces and feeling trapped were resurfacing from her past. We knew the problems never went away but it was like they had been pushed aside by the Alzheimer's.

The next few days my mum's behaviour just got worse and it started to worry me how confined and trapped she must have been feeling. I felt so bad that I couldn't help because she all of a sudden was behaving like she was trapped in

179

her own mind and it didn't matter whether she was outside or inside she was panicking. We got the urine sample back and it was clear so that was ruled out. Whilst sitting watching a singer one weekend my mum started panicking and pulling at her top again. She went all flustered and I didn't know what to do. I gave her some of my drink but she wouldn't settle, she normally loved watching the singers with me. One of the carers noticed my mum's unsettled behaviour and she came over and took my mum up to her room to change her into a lighter top. When they came back down my mum sat and watched the singer but I could see she was disturbed and not her usual self. When going to see my mum in the mornings I was being informed that she was refusing personal care, she would not have her hair washed, have a shower, or even have her hair brushed. My mum looked so rough and distressed that it was upsetting to see. I kept asking the staff why my mum had started behaving this way and they explained that sometimes after a fall, somebody with dementia could be affected in a negative way. It knocks their confidence and they said that it could have resurfaced her claustrophobia because of feeling stuck when falling, and trapped when she fell out of bed. She would have been lost and confused and traumatised by the two falls in a short space of time. I also felt responsible for getting her hair done a few weeks before, and felt this triggered the state she was in now.

About a week went by and my mum was refusing to sleep in her own bed, refusing to sit at the table to eat like she would normally, and still be objecting to most of her personal care. She got upset every time she saw me and told me that she didn't know why she was getting upset all the time. She was in a constant state of panic. I was going to see my mum most evenings as well as the mornings because I needed to know my mum was OK and I wanted to be there to make her feel better if she was feeling upset and trapped. Some evenings I would get to my mum and she would just cry when she saw me and I would have to settle her and sit with her in her room until she fell asleep. I couldn't just leave her when I could see how upset she was. I was informed by the staff after about a week of trying the second bed guard on the bed that it was probably the reason my mum didn't want to sleep in bed. It was a difficult situation because the bed guard was stopping my mum falling out of bed but she was currently refusing to even get in the bed. They said that they thought my mum felt trapped having two bed guards on both sides of the bed and she probably felt restricted having the one on that was nearest to the bedroom door. So it was agreed, we would take the bed guard off and see how my mum got on. A crash mat was placed on the floor next to the side without the guard and hopefully the fall out of bed was not going to be a regular occurrence. The problem was because my mum's bed was purchased by my dad and was a double divan, it couldn't be made to go any lower to the floor. However, it was an option that if my mum continued to keep falling out of bed and it was setting her back, then we could think about getting a bed that other residents use, where it could be lowered closer to the floor. It was an option but an option we hoped we wouldn't need right now and my mum loves her double bed. She has always slept like a moving starfish and takes up the whole bed, I have visited on occasion when she has been asleep in bed and I cannot believe some of the positions she is sleeping in. she would not be able to do that in a single bed. So we would see how we got on and just make the right decision for my mum and her wellbeing.

After a couple of weeks my mum was sleeping in her own bed again, and was gradually getting back to her old self. She was allowing personal care, eating at the table, smiling, laughing and generally much happier. She would still have moments of feeling a bit hot or claustrophobic, but that feeling has been with my mum for so many years that it was bound to rear its ugly head every now and again. I was just so happy to see her not looking like somebody that was trapped in their own mind and there was nothing that could be done about it.

Just as we were beginning to get back on track with my mum and things were looking up we were hit with another obstacle and this one is currently still happening as I type this chapter. A few months ago a virus called Covid-19 or the Coronavirus was and still is spreading rapidly around the world and unfortunately taking millions of lives. It appeared to be more of a risk for those people with underlying health conditions or the elderly. As the virus first made its way to the UK people had little worry or concern about how catastrophic it could be. However, Alderwood made the decision to close its doors to visitors and unfortunately that meant I couldn't go and see my mum. I was absolutely devastated and it took a few days for me to get my head around it.

My daily routine was gone, I couldn't stop thinking about how my mum must have been feeling. Was she going to be angry towards me for not visiting? Would she remember me when I eventually was able to see her again? Would I see a huge decline in her, when I saw her again? It wasn't long after Alderwood closed their doors that the government put the UK into lockdown. This meant not going out unless essential and this included into other people's homes. I knew that this wasn't going to be a few weeks, I didn't know how long I wouldn't be able to see my mum for but I knew it was going to be a substantial period of time. I felt like precious time with my mum was being robbed from me but I also knew that it was for the best. Alderwood have done absolutely amazingly well in dealing with the situation they have been handed. Due to their strict regime they have in place for staff, and due to their forward thinking and closing the doors to their home earlier than required, all staff and residents have been kept safe and well. Whilst I was unable to visit my mum, I popped by every now and again and dropped some treats off for my mum and cakes and treats for the staff. It was my mum and dads anniversary on 1st May.

I went round and had a few social distancing drinks with my dad in his front garden and I dropped off some baileys, a card from my dad, a card from me, some flowers, socks and some chocolates for my mum outside the home. I asked the staff to ensure she had a drink of her baileys to celebrate her anniversary. The staff were kind enough to send me pictures of her enjoying her glass of baileys and reading her cards. They also once again went the extra mile by putting a photo of my mum and dad into a frame for her. It was a photo I had sent to Nikki, to show my mum. I thought this was so thoughtful and once again showed the exceptional care and thought towards all their residents. Whilst I was unable to see my mum, I had pictures of my mum sent to me and videos of her dancing and enjoying herself. Although it was breaking my heart not being able to spend time with her, I knew my mum was in the very best place and could not be receiving better care anywhere else. I rang up the home a few times to see how my mum was but most of my communication was via text or Facebook and the smile on my mum's face said it all. I purchased my mum some new pyjamas, a new top and some chocolates to let her know I was thinking of her and I also ordered a photo pillow with a photo of myself and a photo of my children on the other side. Unfortunately my mum isn't able to understand the situation and wouldn't understand why I was not visiting. I didn't know whether I would be greeted with a smile and a hug or a cold shoulder when I saw her but do you know what, I would take either just to see her again. Millie, my 5-year-old has asked why we are not seeing nanny, and she understands it's because of the Corona Virus. Alderwood were doing skype calls and facetime calls for family members to speak to their loved ones but I didn't feel this was right for my mum. Her lack of understanding could have led to upset or she would have just walked off and not spoke which would have upset me. She doesn't quite understand talking to somebody on a screen as I have tried it before when my dad was away in Manchester. She spoke very few muddled words and then got up and walked off. I didn't want to upset my mum and myself anymore, being kept apart was bad enough.

The home started some socially distanced meetings for families, whereby I could book a slot to go and visit my mum in the garden, as long as I wear a mask and I keep 2 metres apart from her. However, after talking with Nikki, I once again decided it could possibly do more damage than good with my mum. As she lacks the understanding she wouldn't appreciate being told to stay away from me. I am normally greeted with a hug from my mum but this could not be allowed to happen. Therefore, I felt I was best waiting until I could have a normal meeting with my mum like we used to. I didn't want her wondering why I was wearing a mask and why I was standing away from her. I was holding out hope that it wouldn't be too much longer until I could see my mum and give her a great big hug. It was going to be so emotional, I knew that for sure. I just hoped things were the same as when I last saw her and I hoped our bond was as strong as it was before. I would be devastated if I had lost that connection with her.

After several more weeks I was so desperate to see my mum that I decided to go with the garden visit to see her. It was a day I will never forget. My dad and I got to the home with our face masks on and we waited anxiously in the garden for my mum to be brought to us. When we saw her we were absolutely heartbroken, it was not the meeting we were expecting and we were taken aback by my mum's behaviour and appearance. She was very unsteady on her feet, her back wasn't straight so she was leaning over to one side, she was crying her eyes out, flushed, stressed and her co-ordination was pretty much non-existent. I was so gobsmacked because I knew my mum had been happy because I had seen the pictures. I understood that the lift had stressed her but there was definitely more going on than coming down in the lift upsetting her. Was this the cause of being abandoned by her family for over 4 months? I think sometimes maybe a smile and a laugh masks the hurt and confusion a person with dementia is feeling. I feel so strongly that mentally my mum was shattered and this was due to the lockdown. She looked like she had aged about 30 years, she was clinging onto my dad and crying but also kept thinking she was falling. It was really difficult getting her to sit down on a chair, and she was leaning so far over, it didn't look comfortable for her. I was devastated seeing my mum so distressed and upset. It was so traumatic that I was crying, my dad was crying, a career started crying. My mum didn't seem to respond to seeing us because she was so distressed, and in the end she wanted to get up and walk off. She was so upset and unsteady that I couldn't bear to be in the home anymore. I said I wanted to leave and my dad and I left that day with two crushed hearts, and even more traumatised than we were before.

After the disturbing day meeting my mum and also how upset using the lift made her, it was decided that we could meet my mum inside the home with our masks on. The following day I went for my second visit and this one was so much better and made me grateful for the opportunity given by the home. I was so nervous when the staff member led me towards a room to wait for my mum. As soon as she spotted me her eyes lit up, and she cried tears of joy and ran over to me, giving me the biggest hug. She was overjoyed and so was I, this was the mum I was hoping to be greeted by the first time round. The staff all commented on how happy she was to see me and how they hadn't seen her that happy for a little while. I was quite upset that my mum had possibly declined in health because of my absence. I was also informed that my mum wasn't really settling down well and wasn't eating meals. She wasn't happy to sit down and eat and also wasn't sleeping in her bed. Most days she was eating some snacking food down the corridors and sleeping in a chair. My poor mum, had she felt abandoned? Could our absence really have caused as many changes in my mum that I was witnessing? After talking to the staff it was decided that for my mum's health and wellbeing I would be able to visit her in her room, so that I could ensure she was eating meals and accepting her medication.

After a few weeks, my mum seemed to go from bad to worse, She was refusing food from the staff, some days only eating what my dad or I took in for her, or what we fed her. She could barely stand up or walk without thinking she was falling over. Getting her to sit on a chair could easily take 10 minutes and it took several staff members just to change her into a night dress. My mum just seemed to be really agitated, stressed, anxious and upset. She was only relaxed and calm when my dad or I was there with her. After a few weeks and a review of my mum's medication and changing some around she was a lot more aware of her surroundings. She had purpose again and the staff are able to bath her and change her incontinence pad more easily. However, she was still not eating for the staff and she had also become quite verbally aggressive. We had been informed that she was swearing a lot and talking to herself or somebody that wasn't actually there an awful lot. When we went in daily you could see it in her eyes that she had lost the relationship she had with the staff, she didn't give eye contact, and ignored them when they were around. She got really upset when we saw her and said they were horrible to her. I knew the staff were good with my mum and had no concerns but something had changed in my mum. She wasn't eating or drinking much unless my dad and I did it for her, and she wasn't relaxed or calm without my dad and I with her. Before and during lockdown my mum was happy, smiling, dancing, eating, drinking and taking her medication. Now she was quite angry, unhappy, sometimes refusing her meds and not eating or drinking. My dad and I were having to make sure she was getting her essentials because unfortunately she wasn't happy for the staff to do any of those things for her. After a meeting with Nikki it had been decided that we would change her medications again to see if we could get my mum back to her happy place. My dad and myself really struggled seeing my mum but luckily she was always happy to see us which made it that bit easier. The thing is with Alzheimer's is there is never a simple answer to anything. Nobody can tell us that a decline is due to medication, the Alzheimer's, mental health due to the lockdown or something else. Alzheimer's is so unpredictable and the way it affects people is different for everybody. We were hoping that with the help of the doctors, the home and ourselves we could get my mum back to the lady that was happy and smiling and had a relationship with the staff.

Who knows what my future holds with my mum and who knows what other obstacles we will have to face. I would have never predicted the situation we are in now and one thing Alzheimer's is not, is predictable. From the falls, to the declines, to the good days and the bad, I will face every challenge head on and will always strive to do my best by my mum.

My World Comes Crashing Down

I told you that this book was written over time, so therefore things change. My mum was still struggling with her mental health since the lockdown. I was still going in daily to see her and to make sure she was eating because she was eating very little for the staff. I was going in, washing her hair in a bucket whilst she sat on her chair, I was washing her feet in a bowl and getting as many calories into her as possible whilst I was there. We put music on, we sang, we laughed and my mum was happy. However, I was starting to notice that the medication my mum had been put back on wasn't helping. Her co-ordination was ten times worse again and she was unknowingly pulling herself to the ground a lot. The staff were informing me that my mum was becoming a challenge and they were not really being able to do their job as she wasn't letting them. She was mentally declining and was talking to people constantly that were not there. I could see we were in a real rubbish situation and I just wanted my mum to be the way she was before lockdown. I could see this medication wasn't working but professionals were refusing to take it off her because of her mental state. I wanted to bang my head off a brick wall because it felt like another one of those times whereby those that knew my mum best were being ignored and those that had the qualifications made all the decisions. The care home agreed that this particular medication was not having a very good impact on my mum. It helped slightly with the anger verbally towards the staff but she was still not letting them do anything for her and she was still talking to people that were not there (something this medication should have been helping with). To top it off it was making her walk sideways whilst leaning and meant she had two falls in less than a week. I was really angry that it felt like my mum had no voice and my voice was being ignored. Her quality of life right now was being greatly reduced and it felt like the downward slope she was on had just got a whole lot steeper.

I was sure things could not get any worse for us, but then one morning I got a call to inform me that the care home had its first case of Covid-19 and they would be closing their doors to visitors again. I understood why they had to close their doors but also pleaded, explaining that my mum needed me right now. She wasn't eating properly and she was mentally really unstable. Unfortunately I believe it was out of the care homes hands and they had to follow the advice and rules and stop visits. I was heartbroken. I couldn't believe it was happening again and at such a critical time for my mum. I spoke to my dad about bringing my mum home to be looked after but we both knew realistically that it wouldn't work. My mum would end up walking out the house, falling down the stairs, or touching something hazardous. The list of reasons why she couldn't come home were endless, but I was still so tempted. I had already missed so much time with my mum and I just wanted to be there to care for her and to make her smile. To make things worse, I knew she would be asking for me and wandering where I was again and this broke my heart. When I found out Covid-19 had got into the home I wasn't too concerned, I felt like it would happen at some point and they did well to keep it out for as long as they did. I also felt that my mum was one of the youngest residents, if not the youngest and I felt like if anyone could fight it, it would be her because she was physically a lot fitter than most residents in a care home. However, I don't think I really knew how bad it was and how it affected people.

A few days later I was due to have a socially distanced visit outside with the social worker Hayley and Nikki, so we could discuss how my mum was doing and what we thought we should do to help. I was sat in my car and I got a call from Hayley and she had an important update for me. She asked if I had spoken to Nikki and I said no, so she went on to tell me that my mum had tested positive for corona virus. I cannot actually explain how I felt at that moment in time. It was like my mum was having to climb brick walls and each time they were getting higher and higher. It felt like she was being handed the worst luck and I just wanted things to be better for her. I again was not too concerned for my mum, but I just thought she did not need to feel rubbish on top of the challenges she was having with her medication and her mental health. It was just another obstacle and to make it worse this time, I couldn't be there to help her or reassure her. I offered to work for the care home so that I could see my mum, I offered to volunteer and help, my dad offered to isolate with my mum in her room, we were desperate. Desperate to be with her and make sure she was OK. All of our suggestions and concerns came to nothing because of the rules in place and it just felt like we were in a helpless situation.

A few days later we had a video call with Nikki, Hayley and the consultant who dealt with my mum. I was at my dad's house and did most of the talking and listening but my dad also briefly said his piece. The consultant seemed to have empathy towards us about wanting to be there to care for my mum but Nikki was adamant that due to the rules from public health we could not go into the home. My dad and I argued our case and said that my mum needed us and she was in a bad way with her mental health and who knows what a second period of time without us would do to her but unfortunately it didn't matter, the rules were the rules. We learned that my mum was on diazepam to calm her because she needed to stay in her bedroom as she couldn't be allowed to roam the corridors and spread the virus. I understand them not wanting to spread the virus but couldn't understand how they would keep somebody like my mum in her room, when she would normally spend a lot of her day walking up and down. Also with my mum's claustrophobia I didn't feel happy about her being restricted. However, the rules were the rules and there was not much I could do or say to change things. I just felt like the diazepam would react badly with my mum. I had seen her after taking one tablet and she was very sleepy and slurring her words. It was like it made her more incapable than she already was which I don't agree with when her capabilities were already being slowly destroyed by the Alzheimer's. I knew they needed to do it and understood why but from my point of view it was upsetting and slightly immoral. It angered me but at the same time felt like it was the only option if me or my dad were not able to help. I could not understand why my dad could not isolate with my mum in her room and therefore take care of her and help with her mental decline. She was now having medication that was upsetting her, being made sleepy and slow, stuck in her room, with no family and all whilst fighting a virus and also living with Alzheimer's. I also hated thinking about how my mum must have been feeling or what she was thinking. I had been by my mum's side every single time she needed me. Each time she went to hospital, into a home, to the doctors, appointments and each and every day and now I couldn't be there. This absolutely killed me inside, it still does now. By the end of the telephone call it was decided my mum's medication would stay the same which I wasn't happy about, and my dad and I were not going to be able to support my mum. I was nearly in tears and my dad just said to Nikki that he trusted they would care for my mum and look after her and understood she was following the rules. Nikki informed us that my mum was asymptomatic with the Covid-19 and she said she would keep us updated. I was really happy that it appeared the virus wasn't affecting my mum but at the same time I still felt like my mum needed her family now, more than ever and I hated the thought of having to leave her on her own again.

A day later I received a couple of videos from the care home to show my mum's mental health and how bad it was. It showed her talking to herself a lot, but from my perspective as her daughter she looked quite distressed and upset. In the videos her hands were shaking, she looked really confused, she looked dishevelled, and she starts crying. She was also asking where I was which absolutely tore me apart. Obviously I wanted to work as a team with the professionals and the care home. We all wanted to get my mum better and this was why the videos were taken because the consultant and social worker were unable to see my mum in person. However, I was really angry at being kept away from my mum when she quite clearly needed me, I was angry at the rules. I felt like my mum was an exception, she was unwell, she was declining, the first lockdown impacted her negatively and she was making the staffs job difficult. If the staff couldn't do what was required because my mum wasn't letting them, then I could. I was emailing Hayley, texting Nikki, I even emailed the local councillor to see if he could help and he was kind enough to reply and said he had emailed the relevant person. I just couldn't understand why I was being kept from my mum when it was quite clearly only my dad and I that could meet her basic needs properly. She was only happy and smiling when we were there, otherwise she was distressed and being problematic for the staff. She was declining rapidly with her mental health and physical state. It was only a week or so ago that I was feeding her milkshake making her laugh and smile and now she was upset, scared and in a dark place without me. I was doing all I could to be there for my mum and to get somebody to listen to me.

The next day I got a call that would turn my whole world upside down and make me feel a hurt and pain I had never ever felt before in all my life, and I didn't think that was possible after the tough few years I had got through. It was Nikki from the home and she told me that my mum had taken a turn for the worst. She explained that her breathing had been affected and that she felt she might need to go to the hospital. She told me to go to the home and I could see my mum and make the decision with them. I instantly knew it couldn't be good, as they were allowing me into the home and I wasn't allowed into the home unless things were really bad. I told Nikki I would be there in 10 minutes because I was near the care home anyway and I hung up. I was actually up at the hospital about to pick my dad up after a small procedure. I was crying my eyes out and pulled up outside the exit whilst I waited for my dad. He came out a few minutes later and I burst into tears again and told him what I knew. He was as upset and distraught as I was but he said he couldn't see my mum suffering. We decided to drive to the home and my dad would then take the car with Charlotte and go to the coffee shop a few minutes away. He told me to keep him informed and drove off. I stepped into the foyer of Alderwood and the staff gave me all the full PPE to wear so that I was safe from spreading or catching the virus. I nervously walked round and up the stairs with the staff member to my mum's room. As I got into her room and saw her in her bed I was horrified at what I was seeing. I cried so much my glasses were steaming up and my facemask was sopping wet through. I was absolutely distraught. I went over to my mum who was laying there in a top and a nappy, and she was completely unfocussed. Her eyes were staring into an empty space, she didn't respond to me being there by looking at me or facing me, her body was there but she wasn't. She was grasping for breath and the top half of her chest was moving in and out. She had her mouth wide open and her lips looked really dry. She looked panicked and distressed but at the same time unaware because she wasn't reacting with her eyes or her limbs. I kept saying, 'why is she like a cabbage,' over and over again. I was angry because the last time I saw my mum lifeless and unfocussed it was when she was on medication that was having adverse effects. Now here I was again but this time I knew my mum had the corona virus and I didn't know what was going on. I hadn't been able to be with my mum for 2 weeks and this meant I was in the dark. I was holding my mum's hand one minute and telling her it was going to be OK and then walking off the next crying my heart out. I felt broken, crushed, devastated. I was angry, angry at being stripped of the last 2 weeks with my mum. She had been left by us once again and look at what she was going through. My head was all over the place. The home decided to ring for an ambulance so I frantically rang my dad to let him know what was happening. I normally tried to protect my dad from situations that I knew would upset him but he had to know what was happening and there was no hiding from what was going on. I sobbed down the phone to him, I told him it wasn't good news and that mum was in a bad way. I asked him if he wanted to swap with me because he may not be able to see her otherwise with all the Covid-19 restrictions in place but he said he couldn't. I totally understood how he felt, and knew he would be heartbroken to see my mum laying there struggling for every breath, coughing, her eyes fixated with no reaction. I got off the phone and went back over to my mum. She was gasping for breath but was unable to take fluid via a syringe, she just coughed with even the smallest amount and it was as if she was choking on it. A moment that will never leave me and haunts me still now is when my mum coughed a few times and started struggling for breath more. She then gasped and muttered the words, 'I can't breathe.'

I said to the deputy manager who was on the phone to 999, 'did she just say she can't breathe?' And she nodded. I was so distressed by this because it was always a nightmare of my mum's to not be able to breathe. In a way I was relieved that the Alzheimer's appeared to make her less aware or less frantic but at the same time my heart was in pieces. I hated seeing my mum suffer and this was the most traumatic image I had ever seen. I felt for the first time that there was nothing I could do. I also felt guilty and like I had let her down. I should have been with her, nobody should have to get into a state like she was without their family. I just kept thinking about how scared and abandoned she must have felt.

About 10 minutes later the paramedics arrived and they began to check all of my mum's vitals. Her oxygen levels were low so they wanted to give her some oxygen. As they went to place the oxygen mask over my mum's mouth she became frantic and started to panic. She began throwing her arms around and breathing heavier. This was again her claustrophobia causing problems once more, she hated anything over her mouth. However, it did surprise me that she was aware of this considering she didn't appear to be responding very well. I went over to my mum and I held the mask to her mouth and kept telling her over and over again that everything would be OK. Unbelievably my mum responded to this and became more relaxed. This gave me comfort in knowing that she was listening to my voice and hopefully she knew I was there for her. She let me hold the mask to her face and her oxygen levels began to improve. I just kept telling her that everything would be OK as I stroked her face trying to let her know that I was still there. It upset me to see her so panicked and once again in a situation that she probably did not understand. I felt helpless, I just wanted to make her OK. There was absolutely no way I would be leaving my mum on her own so I asked the ambulance guys if I could go with them and they agreed as I was my mum's carer and off we went to hospital. My mum just laid there with the mask on breathing so heavily. I sat there next to her with tears streaming down my face and holding her hand tightly. I couldn't quite believe what was happening. Nikki told me before I left the home that my mum was a fighter and would be OK, she said she was young and someone older had fought it and made it back out of hospital and into the home again. So I knew it would be hard, but I held onto hope that my mum was going to be OK.

When we got to the hospital I wasn't allowed in with my mum, I was sat on a chair outside the Covid-19 ward. My friend Serena who is a paramedic came and sat with me and asked if I was OK. She asked the hospital staff for updates and got me some painkillers as my head was pounding. I was so angry that again I couldn't be with my mum, she had Alzheimer's and needed care. I kept thinking about how scared she would be on her own. The doctor came over and asked for a history of my mum, so I told him as much as I could. He told me she was stable and Serena gave him my number so that he could ring me if there were any changes. I decided after a few hours that there wasn't much I could do. I was sat on a chair in a corridor and if I couldn't be with my mum then I should go home and get some rest. So I rang my sister who had been updated by my dad and she came and collected me from the hospital. As soon as I left the hospital my upset turned to anger. I got the on the phone to Hayley the social worker and vented all my frustrations. I told her that people needed to start listening and my mum was coming off these medications that I knew were not doing her any good. I said I wanted things to change and I would not be having my mum suffer like this ever again. She was very kind, empathetic and reassuring with her words. She listened and let me vent my anger which is what I needed to do. Not with her, but with everything. The whole situation. I was angry that my mum was in hospital on her own, I was furious that my mum had been suffering and I wasn't there for her and I was adamant I would make a change.

The Last Time We Say Goodbye

That night I was so uneasy, fearful, troubled and couldn't get the image of my mum suffering out of my head. I just kept seeing her lying in bed, gasping for breath and looking confused, lost and scared. I lay in bed thinking about the uphill battle we had to face but I was adamant things were going to change. The next morning, I got a call from the hospital. They informed me that my mum was agitated and needed calming down. I knew the hospital were not allowing visitors but I suggested I go to the hospital and help calm my mum. I said I was able to help her and she needed her family. The man on the phone agreed so I put some clothes on and jumped in the car to make my way to my mum. I was under the impression my mum was awake and probably panicking because of the oxygen mask or not knowing where she was or who the people were around her. I just thought I would be able to sit with her, like I did for the ambulance crew and just calm her down so that she wasn't panicking. I knew if she was panicking that wouldn't help with her breathing. I rang my dad on the way to let him know what was happening and I told him I would keep him updated.

I pulled up at the hospital and quickly found the ward specifically for patients with Coronavirus. I had my facemask on and went to the reception desk and they were aware I was coming. They didn't say anything and just gave me a plastic apron, a face shield and gloves to put on. I was told a doctor would be round shortly and the nurse took me to the door of the room my mum was inside. As they opened the door I took a step inside and I couldn't believe what I was seeing. I broke down in tears and fell to my knees. My mum was not frantic like I thought, she wasn't responding like I imagined. She was laying there in a bed, lifeless in every way except her chest breathing in and out with an oxygen mask on her face. Her eyes were open but not moving, it was like her body was there breathing but the rest of her was gone. I stood up, removed my face shield because it was steaming up, and took my mum's hand. Through tears and heartbreak I asked her if she could hear me. I just kept saying, 'Mum, can you hear me? It's Natalie. I'm here now, can you hear me. Please mum if you can hear me squeeze my hand.' I got no response. I was completely shocked that I thought my mum was distressed and awake when she was completely unresponsive.

A few minutes later a doctor came into my mum's room and introduced himself. He explained that my mum was on steroids, fluids and oxygen and that she was not in a good way. He explained that she had a chest x-ray done the night before and that was very bad. One of her lungs showed a complete shadow and the other side wasn't great either, which meant her lungs were not working very well. He didn't seem to have any positive information for me and seemed quite bleak so I asked him bluntly what was happening and was my mum going to be OK? That's when I heard the words I never dreamt I was going to hear, not yet. Not now! He said, 'look at your mum, she is not well at all. She's unresponsive and she is in a really bad way. I think you should prepare for the worst.'

I couldn't quite believe what I was hearing. I was expecting my mum to be annoyed, confused and stressed about being in hospital. I did not expect to see her laying there unresponsive. My whole world had just been shattered and I felt alone, guilty, heartbroken, and like I had nothing left. I was completely destroyed by this news and straight away thought about how my dad was going to react. However, I needed to clarify what the doctor was telling me. Through tears and anguish, I asked him, 'Is there a chance my mum could pull through?'

He replied with, 'no, your mum is not going to get better.' He then went on to inform me that if she wasn't showing any signs of improvement by the next day then they would take away the steroids and fluids because she didn't need them. He told me I should inform my family and they could come up and see my mum. I knew instantly that this doctor knew my mum was not going to pull through, because he would not allow family onto the Covid ward otherwise. For a small moment, my life wasn't worth living, I forgot about my kids, my husband and everybody else. My mum was dying and there was nothing I could do to help. Through the last few years there was always something I could do to help, but not this time. I was utterly inconsolable and I felt numb with pain. I managed to find the strength to ring my dad and told him the earth-shattering news. I could feel his pain through the phone, and he was undecided whether he could see my mum or not. My aunty Sue was also down with my cousin so I knew she would be able to persuade my dad to come and see my mum before it was too late. Although I always tried protecting my dad from whatever I could, I felt he should at least come and say goodbye to my mum no matter how hard it was. I then rang my sister and told her and she said she would come to the hospital right away. I told her to drop her children to Shaun and then come to the hospital. None of us were expecting this, we were all shell shocked. Although my mum had Alzheimer's I don't think we realised how cruel the Corona virus was and just how bad it could be.

I sat with my mum and was willing her to give me a sign that she could hear me or that she was aware of me being there but I was getting nothing. I held her hand tightly and just tried to prepare myself for not getting the chance to hold her hand ever again. This woman meant the world to me, she was my best friend, my mum, I saw her most days even before her diagnosis of Alzheimer's and I was not ready for her to leave me. Not yet! I had prepared for the decline, for her to be bed ridden, for her to forget who I was. I wasn't prepared for this. I was so angry that my mum just seemed to be given one bad day after the other and nothing seemed to ever go right for her since her diagnosis. I could not imagine a life without my mum in it, she was such a huge part of my life. A few minutes later, whilst my thoughts were running wild, my sister walked through the door. She broke down in tears and we cried together. She hadn't seen my mum for about 7 months and now she was seeing her dying in hospital. It honestly felt like this wasn't how it was supposed to be. We sat and spoke about what was happening and I told her what the doctor had told me. A few minutes later my dad, aunty and cousin walked in. My dad was absolutely heartbroken. He told me and my sister to go outside so we went for a walk and a breath of fresh air. I know my dad and how he copes and I knew he wouldn't want us sat there whilst he was upset, and I knew he would want time to himself with my mum so he could talk to her, like I did when I was on my own with her. We were outside for about 5 minutes when my aunty appeared and she told us that my dad had told her to go home. He said there wasn't anything she could do, and she should just go home. We all understood why he was saying that because we didn't really know how much time my mum had and it was just a waiting game. My dad would want his own time to grieve and wouldn't want anybody in the house whilst he did. I told my aunty to hold fire whilst I spoke to my dad just to make sure it was what he wanted and I said I would text her. She sat down and waited whilst me and my sister made our way back to the ward to see my dad. I spoke to my dad and it was quickly decided that my aunty should go back home whilst it was still light because my dad felt there was nothing more she could help with. We all understood his wishes and I text my aunty and she headed back to Manchester with my cousin that day. She felt glad she had the chance to say goodbye to my mum and my dad and I really appreciated her coming down for support in the first place.

Whilst the three of us sat with my mum we asked someone to get a doctor so that we could clarify what was happening and also so my dad could hear it for himself. A few moments later a doctor knocked on the door and asked how he could help. My dad asked if there was any chance my mum could get better or pull through this and the doctor said no, he went on to say that my mum was dying. We asked why she was still on fluids and steroids if she was not going to get better and the doctor said that those could be stopped if that was what we wanted. As a family we decided that there was no need for the steroids and fluids if my mum was dying. My dad made it very clear to the doctor that we did not want to see my mum in any pain or discomfort so the doctor agreed that my mum would be placed on end of life and would receive palliative care. This would include regular morphine injections so that my mum would be comfortable. We all agreed and the doctor said he would get someone to come and sort all of that out. It was such a difficult decision because to me it felt like we were taking my mum's essential things away from her, but the doctors were going to do it the next day anyway. Also the doctor had no doubt my mum was dying and therefore it felt it was only right that end of life was started rather than prolonging the agony for my mum and for us. All I kept thinking was that if my mum was aware of what was going on, in any way at all then she wouldn't want to prolong it. She wouldn't want to be fighting for breath for longer than she needed to. It was absolute torture for me. Seeing her chest rise up and down, with no other sign of life, no response. It wasn't just going to torment me for the next few days but for the rest of my life.

After speaking to the doctor and sitting with my mum for an hour or so, the realisation of what was happening finally hit. My mum was going to pass away but nobody could tell us when. There was absolutely no way I was leaving my mum on her own again, so my sister and I decided we would be staying by my mum's bedside until the time came. My dad said his goodbyes and went home possibly thinking that would be the last time he saw my mum, but that wasn't to be the case. She went into hospital in the evening on Friday 23rd October 2020 and a couple of days went by with what felt like not much change. My sister and I sat with my mum and had no sleep for the 2 days that had passed. We were both sick with anticipation, waiting with nerves curled up in our stomachs. My dad stopped by each day, I don't think he expected it to be so prolonged. My sister and I went home on the Saturday to walk the dogs and clear our minds, whilst my dad sat with my mum holding her hand. By the Sunday we were like zombies. Tired, tormented and upset zombies. I was texting my paramedic friend sending her videos of my mum's breathing because I thought she could give me an insight into what was happening. One minute she was a few seconds between breaths and the next there was a few more, then it became rapid, and then it changed again. I was trying to work out what was happening. I kept counting in my head over and over again. I was doing it so much that I was doing it without realising it and I was picking up on any small changes. 1,2,3,4,1,2,3,4 over and over in my head. I hated not knowing and this was giving me anxiety like I have never experienced in my life. Watching my mum breathe, waiting for her to take her last. It was torture. For the whole weekend, my sister and I stayed with my mum. We chatted, we laughed, we cried, we asked a lot of questions. Every time a new nurse in charge introduced themselves we asked them what was happening. We questioned my mum's state, we asked how long she had left, we asked questions on how we would know if my mum was near to taking her final breaths. It was so frustrating because nobody knew. My mum was unresponsive, but her breathing seemed so strong and like it could go on forever. I kept questioning our decision to start her on end of life because it felt like she was fighting and not giving up any time soon. Should we have kept her on the fluids and steroids so she had a fighting chance? Was she so unresponsive because of the morphine? Had we given up on her too early? Every single time a doctor came into the room I got my dad or my sister to question what was happening again. I needed to be sure that my mum was dying and this wasn't questionable. I had seen my mum unresponsive before and that was due to medication so I didn't want the doctors confusing my mum's unresponsive state with her reaction to the virus when it may possibly have been a concoction of all the medications she was on, the virus, the morphine and the Alzheimer's. I needed to be sure. My sister and I saw my mum's legs flinch a few times and this was disturbing, we did not want her to be in pain or aware of what was happening. It was decided that she would be administered morphine through injection as well the pump she had in her leg. Every now and again I had questions that were giving me reasons to doubt what was happening. I started questioning the morphine and the effects this was having on her responsiveness. I thought what if she could be improving but the morphine was making her unable to respond? I think I was in denial that my mum was dying and I was looking for any other reason. However, I also didn't want to be making decisions that would possibly shorten my mum's life if she had any chance of survival. I was told several times by doctors, nurses, my dad and my sister but I couldn't stop the doubt running through my head. However, when I looked at the reality of the situation, I had to listen to the professionals.

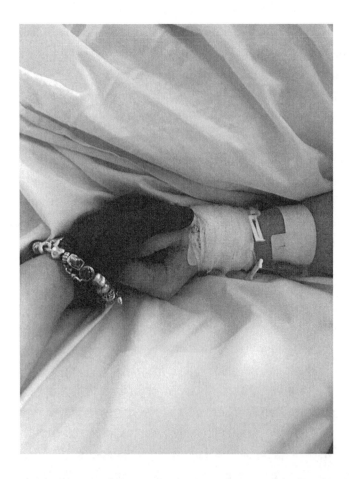

Two whole days and nights passed by slowly and painfully. My sister and I tried to sleep on chairs, on the hard floor with a coat as a cover and a bag as a pillow, but nothing worked. I have never been able to keep my eyes open for as long as I did. Looking back I don't know how I managed, must have been the anxiety and stress keeping me awake. One minute we were telling stories about my mum and laughing about the past, having a joke. The next minute we were sat in silence just staring and thinking about what was actually happening. We were eating snacks and sweets to keep our energy levels at some sort of normal, and drinking energy drinks to try and keep our eyes open, but instead felt like they made my anxiety worse and gave me more of a headache than I had started with. I felt like I was going mad and the world I was in was not a reality. At one point my sister was talking to me about something and it made me laugh so hard. I was laughing so much that tears filled my eyes, I was hysterical. A few seconds later that laugh turned into a devastated cry and I was whaling my eyes out. My sister looked at me in disbelief and questioned whether I was laughing or crying. I said I didn't know and started laughing again hysterically. That soon turned to upset again and I was sobbing my heart out. This continued for about 5 minutes and I couldn't stop. If anybody would have walked in I'm sure they would have thought I needed professional help. I didn't know what I was doing, I couldn't stop and I didn't know how I felt. I felt guilty for laughing, I felt stupid for crying. I kept trying to hold myself together but that didn't go too well. Anytime I was left on my own with my mum I broke down so I told my sister not to leave me and not to go to the toilet. Every time I was on my own the situation became real and I couldn't cope. When the staff came in to change my mum and wash her, we waited outside and it filled me with dread. When we went back into the room, my mum looked slightly flushed and her breathing pattern changed. It seemed to be stressing my mum out even though she couldn't express this.

My dad had a religious lady come into my mum's room whilst me and my sister were not there. I personally didn't see the point in this but I know it made my dad feel better. My mum wasn't really religious and neither am I. However, on the Sunday whilst me and my sister were sat talking the religious lady came in because my dad had asked her to. He felt it would make us feel better. I know this is going to sound really selfish but I was angry that she was in my mum's room and angry that I felt I needed to be polite and go along with her presence and what she wanted to say. I was sat on the floor at the time because my back was hurting, and my sister was sat opposite me. The lady was very polite and kind, but she was very religious and I didn't feel it was appropriate for myself or my mum. She asked if I wanted to say anything and I said no. I was grieving for my mum and I wanted to do this privately. She placed some beads in my mum's hand and then after saying a few words she left. When she said her few words it slightly upset me because it was like my mum was gone already. She spoke about her in the past tense and I wasn't ready to hear this, not yet. Not whilst she was still alive and breathing in front of me. My dad also left a white religious bear by my mum's head on her pillow before he left. I wanted to throw the bear out of the window because I just kept thinking my mum wouldn't want it there because it was an ugly old bear and she wasn't religious. I couldn't move it though, as it was my dad's idea and it meant something to him. I just kept looking at the bear, like it was the bears fault for being in my mum's room when it shouldn't be.

After two very long stressful and upsetting days and nights Monday morning was here. By this point we were all mentally and physically exhausted. I felt like I was going to have a heart attack every time my mum's breath wasn't the same as the one before. Watching her upper chest move in and out for so long was absolute torture. Knowing she was dying and knowing she was struggling, it was so tough just sitting there watching when there was nothing I could do to help. My dad arrived at the hospital nice and early and we decided we needed to talk to somebody. We felt like we had just been left to our own devices in the hospital, nobody was coming in very often to check on us, or my mum. It was decided the palliative care team would get involved and we were told they would come and see us in a short while. The consultant from the palliative care team and another lady knocked on my mum's door and came in. I think they were quite surprised with how long my mum had been going for and also how obvious and loud her breathing was. I was expecting my mum to breathe very lightly and quietly and eventually pass peacefully but this wasn't happening. I didn't know what I should have been waiting for, what to expect or what was going to happen and that scared me so much. The palliative care team at the hospital were amazing. They were caring, informative, sincere and empathetic. They answered all our questions and made me feel like I understood what was happening a little bit more. They couldn't tell me everything I needed to know because they said everybody was different in this situation but they were there for us and made us feel supported. They got a nurse from there department to sit with us to reassure us and make us feel like we were not on our own which was amazing. My dad, my sister and I had decided between us that we would ask why my mum was on oxygen if she was dying. We wandered whether that was making this suffering for us all much longer than it needed to be. We asked the consultant if the oxygen was delaying the inevitable and she said yes. She informed us that the oxygen would be helping my mum and keeping her going longer. We asked if it was possible to take her off the oxygen. Now some people may think why would you want to take the oxygen away when its keeping her alive, but we saw it as freeing my mum and ourselves from the torment. Sitting day in day out with my mum fighting for each breath was agony, it broke my heart. If my mum had any sort of awareness that she was struggling for her breath It would have been awful for her too. It was breaking me watching her and I just wanted her to be peaceful and calm. If there was absolutely any chance of her fighting and surviving then I would have been with her every step of the way, no matter how awful it was to see. Every single professional we spoke to told us that my mum was dying and she would not make it. The consultant spoke with somebody at another hospital and it was decided that my mum could come off the oxygen. This really upset me but I knew it was for the best. The consultant explained how as doctors they are not allowed to purposely take somebodies life but as my mum was already dying, then taking the oxygen away was in her best interests. We explained my mum's fear of not being able to breathe and her claustrophobia and I knew that my mum wouldn't want to suffer anymore. If I was in her shoes and I had no chance of survival then I wouldn't want myself or my family to suffer for any longer than they had to. They explained how they would give more morphine and other medications to help my mum and assured me she would be comfortable. I believe they could see the pain in our eyes and they wanted to help us. The consultant believed my mum wasn't aware of what was going on which was reassuring to hear. Once the decisions had been made my dad said his goodbye and my sister and I sat and waited for the plan to be put into action.

The palliative care team were true to their word and were with my sister and I every step of the way for the entire day. They asked if we needed food, they got us an overnight bag with a few things in, they even got us a mattress to put on the floor so that we could get some sleep. They sat and spoke to us about my mum and the lady she was, showing care and interest. The consultant then went on to inform us that it was time for my mum's oxygen to be lowered. She explained how she was going to lower the oxygen every 20 minutes so that it wasn't such a big change like if we just took the oxygen away completely straight away. She reassured me and my sister that the decision was hers and not ours and although I knew she was saying this to make us feel better, she assured us that it was the right thing to do. My stomach was doing summersaults. I didn't know what to expect, I was apprehensive and sick with the knowledge that this was really happening. She removed the oxygen mask from my mum's face and replaced it with a different one. She then sat with us to wait for any change. She didn't leave us alone, she made me feel like we had support and although I was sick with dread, I felt easy knowing somebody that knew what they were doing was present. A little while later she did the same again. Removed the mask and replaced it. This time as she did this, my mum's breathing pattern changed dramatically. We all looked at each other in a horrified state wandering what was going to happen. The consultant told me and my sister to sit next to my mum. We sat holding her hand crying our eyes out. My whole world was collapsing in front of me. I felt like I wasn't prepared for this. After nearly three days of sitting in her room and waiting, I still was not ready. We sat not knowing what was going to happen and I believe the consultant thought that my mum was going to pass away, however this was not the case. My mum continued with this new breathing pattern for a while longer. I was really relieved but I also knew that although it didn't happen that time my mum was going to stop breathing at some point and I couldn't get my head around that. From that point on, my stomach felt like it was on the ground and my heart was aching so much it felt like I needed to be using the oxygen available. I asked the consultant how we would know when it was happening. She explained that everyone was different but normally you would begin to see small gaps in the breathing. Like she was holding her breath. Or it would become really quiet and then she would just take her last breath. I felt like it was just a really horrible, tormenting waiting game. My mum's eyes had become glazed over at this point, it was becoming difficult to look at her face. Her mouth open, her pupils fixated, and her eyes with a tinge of yellow. Her mouth was dry and she looked tired. A little while later the consultant was back to lower the oxygen once again. This time there was no change. After about 20 minutes the consultant returned and explained that she was now going to remove the oxygen mask completely and that she would wait outside the room for about 30 minutes. However after this point she would be going home, so she gave us the phone number for the palliative care team and also another hospital that could answer any questions if we had any. I was really anxious and scared of being on our own again, also apprehensive about the removal of the oxygen completely. Would my mum gasp for breath without it? Would she stop breathing straight away? The consultant explained that she wasn't expecting anything dramatic to happen straight away. She gave us a caring reassuring look with her eyes and then removed the mask. I was so nervous I felt like I was no longer in control of my own body or how I felt. I didn't know what to expect but nothing changed apart from the volume of my mum's breathing because the mask wasn't shielding it. It was strange to see her whole face without the mask, but she continued with her big breaths in and out. We thanked the consultant and I truly believe her and her team made a huge difference for us that day. I felt like a child, scared, vulnerable and alone and the consultant helped us feel a bit more supported on the worst day of our lives. Now it felt like a waiting game so we sat and stared at my mum so closely trying to notice any change at all.

After about an hour I was feeling so apprehensive, lifeless, lost, confused. I didn't know what was happening, what to expect, when it was going to happen and I think all these questions were deflecting from the actual fact that very soon I would be without my mum. It never really occurred to me that I would never hold my mum's hand again, I would never see her face again, never see her smile again. I was so focussed on what was happening right in front of me. Hoping she was not suffering, praying she was not aware, eager for this torture to end. Seeing my mum breathing so loudly, knowing she was dying was agony, as was seeing her body slowly shutting down. I wanted to block out the noise and close my eyes. I knew this moment was going to stay with me for the rest of my life and it was not going to be comforting for me. My sister and I kept speculating how much longer my mum was going to be able to breathe for without the oxygen when it was obvious her body was being overworked, exhausted and pushed to its limits. A short while later, we started to notice my mum's breathing pattern change slightly. She was having a small delay between inhaling and exhaling every now and again. We didn't really know what this meant but looked at each other anxiously. It wasn't long before these pauses in her breathing were becoming more frequent. I think we both knew by this point that this was the change the consultant was talking about and when she said we would know when it was happening, this is what she meant. We sat, we sobbed, we looked closely at my mum. I started to question whether I could cope with the situation and whether I needed to be there until the end. However, I just could not bring myself to leave my mum, not when I had never left her before. The pauses in breath were now happening after every time she inhaled. We sat on the edge of our seats waiting for her to exhale her breath. The pauses got longer and longer, and for us more painful. Waiting for my mum to take that breath out was the most painful, insufferable most unbearable wait I had ever experienced.

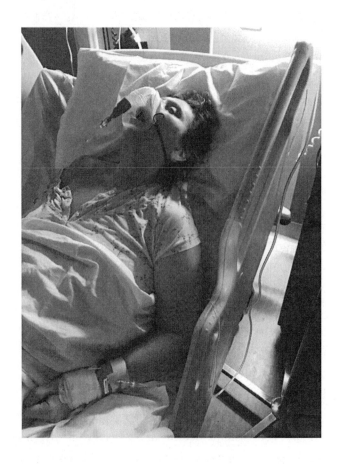

A few minutes later my mum took a few very long pauses in between her breathing and we both said to each other, it's happening. We sat there sobbing, tears running down our faces, our mind and soul crushed. Then after several days of heartache, anger and confusion, my mum drew her last breath. We sat and stared waiting for her to exhale and it never happened. Suddenly all the emotion I thought I had released throughout this horrific time came flooding out and I was inconsolable. My sister and I let out a huge whale of disbelief, upset and heartbreak. My world had stopped, my heart was in two and my body was in shock. Some people would say that it was a relief and I thought I would feel relieved it was all over but I didn't. I wanted to hear that awful, loud breathing again. I wanted to see her chest moving, I needed my mum. I knew from that moment on I was going to miss that woman so much, and I knew that I was not over the worst of how I felt. That day on Monday 26th October 2020 I lost my best friend, the only person I could ever go to no matter what. The world lost one of the kindest, most loving people that has been lucky enough to walk it.

The Conclusion
The Good, The Bad, and The Ugly

Throughout my mum's entire journey with Alzheimer's and her death we have been on a rollercoaster of emotions. Unfortunately, I feel most of them emotions have not been positive ones and my mum's battle was a tough one to say the least. Nobody can say they behaved perfectly, including myself. There were moments of anger, moments of frustration and sometimes we all showed our bad and ugly side. It has been a whirlwind of emotions for me. Everybody deals with grief or upset differently and I hide away from talking about how I feel. I don't want to talk to people about my feelings and I know that probably won't help in the long run but I just cannot help wanting to lock myself away and dealing with how I feel on my own. I don't think people will understand how I feel, I don't think most people are that interested because at the end of the day I feel people have their own lives and own problems. I used to speak to my aunty in Manchester several times a week when my mum was poorly. I told her everything that happened but I never really spoke about how I felt in depth. If I sat down and spoke about my feelings I would have been in tears and people would have thought I needed help, but I disagree. I needed my mum and nothing was going to bring her back. My aunty was a godsend when I needed to vent, or needed help with a dilemma or just needed to talk about anything. She was usually my first port of call with a lot of my decision making regarding my mum because she is level headed and helped me to make a sensible decision rather than an emotional and swayed one. I am very much somebody who's ruled by my heart when it comes to family and sometimes I need to be reminded to use my head. I talk to my friend Kerry about general things regarding my mum but again never talk about my feelings because I don't want to get upset when I know my upset cannot be fixed. I also feel like people have their own lives and worries and I don't want to inconvenience people with how I feel when it's not for them to think about. People want positivity in their lives. When my mum was ill I rarely got upset about it in front of others. I was so stressed and so lost without the mum I had always known and love but people just saw this strong woman dealing with it and taking what life was handing me with a pinch of salt. They never truly understood that I was breaking inside. I felt very alone. I was trying to juggle so many different aspects of my life whilst caring for my mum and making sure my dad was OK. My sister didn't make the best decisions in life and generally runs to me for help when it's needed and my head just feels like it could explode sometimes. I didn't want my mum to ever feel forgotten whilst she was ill and when she moved to a care home and even if she didn't remember if anybody had seen her for a while, I would. The guilt I felt before the virus came along when I had a day that I had not been to see her was upsetting to say the least. I would normally go and see her at least once a day unless I was physically unable to go that day. I only ever missed a handful of days to go and see her before the lockdown and that was due to sickness, a hospital stay with my son, and a Legoland trip with my family. I'm not saying that's the correct way to be and sometimes it exhausted me. I felt my days were passing me by and I had achieved nothing but upset or a headache, but I also felt like it enabled me to know my mum better than anyone and I was there for every single moment she needed me. When my mum first went into Alderwood I was visiting twice a day most days for the first few months. My life was consumed with making sure she was OK and didn't feel let down or abandoned by us. From the very first day my mum went into a home or when she went to hospital I was never ever going to see her left on her own, because the thought of her being left with no visitors broke my heart. Even if it was a 30-minute trip to the shop up the road, a trip to McDonald's for breakfast, a trip to the theatre, a coffee in the morning, watching a show put on by the care home, or just sitting in her room, they were all time spent with my mum, quality time together. This showed in my relationship with my mum, her eyes lit up when she saw me, she remembered me and most importantly she asked for me. She was my one and only mum and I was always going to be there for her. Nobody deserves to be handed a life sentence like she was when she was told she had Alzheimer's. She was the most caring, kindest, warm-hearted person I knew, and her illness brought out the weaker more emotional side to me but it also made me realise I was stronger than I ever thought I was.

My mum's diagnosis and deterioration also brought out all my bad sides, the sides I rarely see. It's also made me realise how different people are when it comes to showing love and care for somebody. My dad was always my mum's best friend and they did everything together. My dad lost the love of his life to this cruel disease way before she passed away. I had to see his heart breaking and my mum act like everything was normal when she brushed past him or refused a kiss. My dad didn't cope very well, but some days were better than others. I don't think he was ever OK even on the days that he appeared OK. They had an unbreakable bond and marriage and for me they were going to be together forever. Unfortunately, Alzheimer's and Covid-19 had other plans and did what nothing else could have ever done, ripped them apart and made them leave each other's sides for the last time. The Alzheimer's cast a shadow over their love for one another at times but it could never take their undying love away from each other. Even on the days my mum was cruel towards my dad it always eventually got forgotten about and my mum was back to asking for my dad, holding his arm lovingly or smiling at him affectionately. My dad was very good at burying his head in the sand. If he could go away for a month he would and if he could avoid a situation he would. He said he couldn't get his head around the whole diagnosis and how rapidly it took hold. I totally understood why he felt that way, he couldn't love my mum any more than he did and his whole world was flipped upside down. However, on occasion myself and my dad would go and visit her or I would pop over and he would snap at me for no reason whatsoever. I'm so used to my dad's moods because of his PTSD but they worsened with my mum's decline. Most of the time I could take it but some days he had no idea one small snap at me caused me to go home in floods of tears. I felt like I was trying my best day in and day out whilst trying to maintain my own life and care for both my parents and then I was given the cold shoulder or shut down when I spoke like I was irrelevant. The worst part of it all was that I was sometimes the punch bag for my dad's emotions and yet my heart was also breaking. She was my mum and she should have been helping me with my kids, giving me advice, coming out to the cinema with me, having a glass of wine with me or just getting excited with me about life and my kids' achievements. All the simple things that people take for granted when they have their mother in their life, I no longer have. I told my mum that Tommy came first in his sports day or that Charlotte got her first tooth and nothing, no reaction or acknowledgement. That's what Alzheimer's did to her, it took her from me and replaced her with a shell of a lady that I became a mother to. What my dad also didn't realise was that his mood impacted my mood and I went home short tempered with my children. I shouted at them for the smallest things and ignored my husband when he walked in from work, because if I didn't, I would cry and I didn't want to cry. I sometimes felt like my head was just about above the water and I was taking in gulps of water and slowly drowning, then another day I was OK and I was treading the water well and keeping myself afloat. I was never out of the water though, I was always surrounded and every day was a struggle. I did understand my dad's moods, I really did because he was a broken man, but I used to wish sometimes he would think about how his actions could impact me and also understand that I was hurting too. I may have seemed to be getting on with it and taking each day as it came, but if I didn't I would breakdown.

Unfortunately, my sister is the polar opposite to me and this has been shown by her choices and decisions regarding my mum. I have felt let down by my sister's loyalties and priorities, family will always come first to me. She's missed out on a great deal regarding happy memories with my mum and time spent with her and unfortunately it was never unnoticed by my mum, the way she behaved towards my sister would reflect this. Without going into too much detail because unfortunately my sister's lack of effort cannot be changed now, I tried to make her realise time was precious but it never changed anything. Now it's too late. I am not saying she hasn't helped at all but it could and should have been so much more. My mum isn't here, nothing will change and I have realised that the anger eats away at me and makes me a bitter person. I don't want to be that person. I want to get on with my life, make my kids happy and make my mum's memory live on in me. She wouldn't want me focusing on the anger. I am a strong believer in not being able to change someone and who they are. You shouldn't have to ask for somebody to show they care or to give their time. These things come naturally to me and I know too many others. If they don't, then I don't think they ever will. As my dad puts it, me and my sister are like chalk and cheese. Very different views, values and morals.

I am far from the perfect daughter but I did my best in making the right decisions and doing the right thing by my mum. Sometimes my feelings got the better of me and when I took my mum out and she was having a bad day it could put me in a bubble of darkness. I am impatient and I struggled to deal with her behaviour. So if I was in a supermarket and she kept walking off because she didn't want to follow me, I would politely ask my mum several times to stay near me. However, it wouldn't take long for me to ask a little bit less politely for her to, 'stop walking off.' I then got annoyed and upset at myself that I had not been so caring towards her when it wasn't actually her fault. I never lost my temper and never would with her but I was sometimes impatient and although I would describe myself as impatient, the anger and upset made it ten times worse.

My mum's family who live in Manchester didn't see much of my mum when she was diagnosed. I understood they were a 5-hour drive away but I would travel the world to be by my daughter's side as many times as life allowed if one of them was as poorly as my mum. I also appreciate people deal with grief and upset differently but I feel it would have been nice for my mum to have people around her that cared. My mum's illness was so time consuming and yes, it inconvenienced my life, yes, I had to work my life around my mum and yes, sometimes I had to do things I didn't really want to do. But I would do it time and time again and wouldn't change that. My aunty Sue came down and spent quality time with my mum and also phoned most days to see how we were and how we were coping; when we weren't coping she came down to see us and stayed a few days. She did what she could considering the distance between us. I don't think people realise the mental strain dealing first hand with somebody with Alzheimer's has. To the world I am fine unless my mask slips but sometimes I am not OK. Mine and my dad's lives were both paused whilst we became carers and nobody apart from us two will ever understand how bad things were. I'm surprised I'm not divorced. I was an absent wife with mood swings that would give a teenager a run for their money. As soon as Shaun got in the door from work I would go round to my parents to make sure they were both OK, to sit with my mum whilst my dad went to the gym or to wash her and get her ready for bed. It got to the point where my children were asking why I was always out at night. I had to explain I was helping Nanny and Granddad and even though it made me feel slightly guilty I just kept thinking that they had their dad at home who is amazing and a fantastic dad and my mum and dad needed me so much more right now. It's not like they never saw me, it was just that I was missing for bed time or before bed time quite often. It still made it difficult because I wanted to do right by everybody and that included my children.

My connection with my dad has grown so strong since my mum's illness and death. I've seen him hurt and cry, and he's told me his thoughts, we have made plans for the future, and the kids absolutely love him. He's really opened up sometimes and we have certainly used each other to help with this situation. I feel like we are the only ones that have been there physically and mentally from the very start. We have been through some really bad times together and also shared some fantastic memories with my mum together. This is something I will hold close to me for as long as I live. My dad has coped as well as can be expected and to be honest I can see the heartbreak in his eyes, I can see the sadness in his actions and I can see the love still burning strong for my mum. I never ever could have imagined life would turn out this way and I will always cherish the fantastic life my mum had before the diagnosis. She was a very lucky lady that lived a fulfilled life with my dad. That's something to ease the pain a little bit.

Memories of my mum before her diagnosis were becoming tainted with the painful image of her becoming a shadow of herself before her death. She looked vacant and she lost the shine in her eyes and the glow in her skin. I looked at pictures of her before she became ill and she looked "alive" and vibrant whereas she became a woman that the life was being sucked out of. Her eyes were empty, her skin had lost its lustre, and her face expressionless for a vast amount of time. 54 was such a young age to be given a diagnosis of Alzheimer's and it made the choices that needed to be made so much harder. Choosing a home for her was such a painful experience because initially I couldn't see past all the old people. It didn't feel right for her to be there. I wanted to write this book to spread awareness. Make people realise that Alzheimer's is so much more than just memory loss, it can hit people younger than 70 or 80 and it affects the family around them so much more than people realise. Being a carer isn't easy especially when you love the person you're caring for so much. If I can help just one person like me with some information or insight into this disease then I will have done something to help. I was told numerous times to speak to somebody online or ring up the Alzheimer's helpline but for me talking to a stranger about my mum who they didn't know wasn't something I wanted to do. However, everybody is different and the help is out there, if talking will help you. There were times I would have liked a bit of insight into what could possibly be the next challenge facing me in regards to my mum, but my advice to anybody is to just do everything you can to help your loved ones. Make them laugh, give them your time and patience and don't forget those helping care for the person with Alzheimer's. They need your support too. I have had support from my friends Kerry and Serena, they helped massively with the children. Enabling me to worry less and be there for my mum. They helped with school pickups, or looking after the children when I have needed them to. It's good to have a cry behind the scenes or with your friends but try to make life for your loved one as comfortable and enjoyable as possible. I have laughed, cried, been angry, scared, but I have no regrets. I am proud of who I am and what I have done for my mum and dad. Something like this has made me realise that life is too short, it's made me realise how important it is to live life to the fullest because you just never know what's round the corner. I didn't miss one appointment with my mum and unless I was physically unable to be there I was always going to be there for her and my dad every day. I love them both so much.

Since my mum's death I have really struggled, more than anyone realises and more than I ever thought was possible. I miss her face so much and I would give anything to hold her hand once again, wash her hair, feed her, sing with her or to see her smile. Memories of the day she died are haunting me every single day, I cannot unsee her chest moving up and down or her face when she took her last breath. Originally my book was finished and my mum was still with me, however I decided I wanted to finish my book including her death. I left it a few months and then decided to finish the ending of my book. It has been hard, reliving it in words but I relive her last moments every single day in my head. I have felt so much anger towards different people about different aspects of my mum's battle but ultimately my efforts will always be focussed on my mum and her memory living on. Not a single day has gone by that I haven't shed a tear for my mum although I hide it well. Every single time I am on my own with nothing to focus on my mind jumps back to her final days. In the car, at night in bed, in the bath or at her graveside. I've felt alone and like my world has caved in around me. My husband doesn't understand how I feel and that makes me feel anger towards him. Although he does everything he can to make me happy, I feel like he thinks I am over it and I am far from being over it. When I'm moody for no reason it's because my brain is filled with upset and images that I cannot remove. I'm back in Alderwood watching my mum coughing and gasping for breath. I am hearing those words over and over in my head, 'I can't breathe.' I keep thinking about the 2 weeks before her death that she was without me and my dad. She was stressed, upset and not happy. We should have been there, I wish I had tried harder. Why wasn't I allowed to be with my mum that Friday evening she went into hospital? She was dying, I should have been there! I am so angry about the whole situation and I feel she deserved more. I have felt very anxious since my mum's death. My heart hurts and my breathing gets heavier. I keep thinking what if I get Coronavirus? I cannot leave my kids without a mum. I am so scared to die and so scared to put my children through what I went through. With Coronavirus still very much present it has made me feel very scared. I have been sat watching the TV and all of a sudden I cannot breathe, I am walking the dogs with my dad and I cannot breathe. My anxiety is through the roof. I feel nervous all the time and apprehensive about what my future holds. I keep thinking about how I told my mum over and over again that everything would be OK. I genuinely believed it at the time too. I am angry that I lied and she was not OK, I just wish I could have made everything OK.

When it was time to plan my mum's burial my dad and I got some of my mum's favourite things and photos placed inside her coffin. My dad told me to put the little white religious teddy into the coffin with my mum and when it came to collecting all her stuff, I couldn't do it. I could not get rid of the ugly teddy that I hated originally. I don't know what it was but I felt that teddy was now special, it was sat by my mum whilst she passed away and I needed it to stay with me. Ironic really, considering I wanted to launch it out the window when my dad brought it into hospital. It now sits on my bedside table and on a few nights I have hugged that teddy whilst crying myself to sleep. I will never ever forget my mum and I hope one day I can look at memories and smile, rather than remembering that awful day she was taken away from me. Sometimes when I hear somebody breathing loudly it takes me back to the hospital sitting watching my mum breathing heavily, fighting for her life. When I hear people talking about the Coronavirus it's a sore topic for me but I just have to get on with it. For anybody that thinks it is no different from the flu, they need to see somebody fighting for their every breath. Only then will they maybe realise that it is so much worse than that.

Every day is a struggle for me at the minute, a struggle I am fighting on my own day in day out. I hope one day I can feel whole again and smile and laugh without feeling guilty. I miss my mum so much and I will never let her memory fade. At the moment nothing makes it any easier, I visit her grave and I don't feel anything but upset and anger. Some people have said that at least she isn't suffering anymore or at least she is at peace but this doesn't help either. Not right now. As far as I'm concerned my mum had just turned 57, she should have been living her amazing life and enjoying many more years ahead of her. She shouldn't have had Alzheimer's and although she did, it doesn't make me anymore at peace with her death. At the moment I need time, time to hopefully be able to remember my mum and smile. We held a memorial for my mum on the 1 year anniversary of her death and it was a lovely day. We felt as a family it had given us enough time to come to terms with what had happened. It was just a handful of my dad's friends that knew my mum, a few of my mums friends, my mums family, my dad's sister and her sons and me, Shaun and the kids. Shaun decorated the venue in a lovely royal blue and we placed photos of my mum around the place. It did feel like we were finally having some sort of send of for my mum and this felt like the closure we needed. With that said I have still not fully come to terms with my mum not being here. I think about her all the time and every family day out or trip leads to me wishing she was with us. One thing is for sure, I will never ever forget you, Mum, and I am hoping your story will bring help to others and comfort in knowing they are not alone.

I love you Mum, with all my heart, and I am so proud of you. Xxx

My Eternal Appreciation

Dad: Thank you for being such a good and devoted husband to Mum. I really didn't think you would cope with Mum's illness as well as you did. I know you found it so tough but you hit every challenge and emotional hiccup head on. Mum loved you so much and I have never seen a woman more in love with any man than Mum was with you. You have done me proud and me and the kids love you so much. Tommy dotes on his grandad and even Charlotte is leaning that way too ☺. We have been through the toughest thing we will probably ever have to face together again. I couldn't have coped as much as I have without you going through it and supporting me the way you have. You have done so much for me, more than anybody will ever know. We have both lost our best friend but she will never ever be forgotten, not while we are still around. I know you have a tough man image to uphold but you're really just a big softy. ☺ You are honest, kind and would do anything for your family. Thank you for being you and not giving up x.

Shaun: I have always said that no man could beat my dad from being the main man in my life. However, as time has passed and with the challenging times I have faced, you have made me realise I have found a man that does everything he can to make me happy. You put me first, ALL the time, you never ever moan about the lack of time I gave you whilst caring for my mum, and you have enabled me to be the best daughter I possibly can. I was able to care for and support my parents and that is all because I have the support of you. I don't know many men that would drive a dinner round to their father-in-law's several times a week before eating their own dinner, or that spends his weekend decorating his father-in-law's house or mother-in-law's new room in her home. I don't know many men that will drive to Manchester and back to pick up a family member to support their father-in-law because times are tough, or that takes annual leave to put a new shower in their father-in-law's house or to support their wife with her mum. You have gone above and beyond what anybody could expect from a husband. You asked me how my mum was every single time I went to see her. The kids and I are lucky to have you. Thank you x. (You best print this out because I won't be this nice again.)

Hayley and Bethany (Social Workers): If I could go back to the beginning and choose a social worker and her assistant, I would choose you both time and time again. You have both been friendly, professional, caring and understanding. You have made me laugh when times were tough and allowed me to cry when I have needed to. You held my baby when my arms were full (feel free to come round and babysit anytime) ☺, you fed my baby her bottle whilst I was trying to help my mum and you have been at the end of the phone anytime for me whether that be by call or email. When times have been tough I have emailed you both and you have always done your best to help in any way. Hayley, over the time you have been my mum's social worker, you became more like a family friend. You got to know us well and as my mum's case has been somewhat eventful you have had a massive input into her welfare. I know my mum's memory wasn't the best but she never forgot who you were when you walked into her house and she greeted you with a, 'what have I done now' type of face ☺. You did your best to give my mum the best, including the home she finally ended up in. That will never ever be forgotten. Without your help things could have been so different and it most definitely would not be for the better. You're amazing at what you do, and thank you! X

Elaine: You have been such a true loyal friend to my parents over the numerous years you have known them. Popping round to see my mum and keeping her occupied whilst my dad was at work. When she became ill you helped my dad and myself wherever possible, coming round to calm my mum, or to just have a cup of tea. I know if I need you and you can help, you will because that's the sort of caring person you are. You went to the care home and spent quality time with my mum once a week and for that I will always be grateful. A true friend you most certainly are ☺. Thank you x.

Nikki and your Alderwood Team: My mum's illness had gone rapidly downhill from the moment she was diagnosed. We had nothing but heartache and upset. When it came to choosing a home it was such a heart wrenching thing to do because I knew that was my mum's final place she would call home. It had to be good enough for her and enable her to enjoy life as much as possible. Alderwood was by far the best home. The staff were friendly, caring and put my mind at ease that she was being looked after the best she could be. There was no way I could have been as much as a part of my mum's life if she was in some of the other homes I looked at because it would have hurt me so much to leave her there. For the most part she was happy and settled in Alderwood and it became a second home for me and my family. So much time and effort is put into the residents in your care, they go on days out, have musicians come in and you celebrate their special days with effort beyond belief for a care home. You really are exceptional and you will never understand the relief you gave me, how you helped me keep my head above the water and enabled me to keep going forward. Nikki, you are kind, caring, and such a down to earth lady. You have an understanding of each and every resident and that is such an important trait to have and cannot be taught. You should be super proud of the home that you manage and never ever change for anybody because you have a heart of gold and that does not go unnoticed. I will never forget the day I came into your home and poured my heart out to you, you listened and showed kindness for my situation. That was a day that truly changed our situation for the better and you gave us some hope for the awful journey my family were facing. Thank you x.